Things That BITE

A REALISTIC LOOK AT CRITTERS THAT SCARE PEOPLE

by Tom Anderson

ADVENTURE PUBLICATIONS, INC.
CAMBRIDGE, MINNESOTA

To Nancy, for your love, support and love bites.

Acknowledgments

Grateful acknowledgments to the many who directly or indirectly made this book possible.

In the summer of 1993, I was paddling on the upper reaches of the Seal River in northern Manitoba on a Science Museum of Minnesota trip with guide and dear friend Cliff Jacobson. The bugs were bad and I jokingly suggested that Cliff write a book on the Basic Essentials of Things That Bite. He waved the mosquitoes from his face, looked at me and said, "No, Tom, that is a book you should write." Since that summer, not a year has passed when Cliff hasn't asked me about the book's progress. So thanks, Cliff, for your urgings, support and confidence. I am hoping we can share more campfires in places where things bite.

This book would not have been possible without the input and suggested species to include from the many frontline naturalists, teachers and biologists across the country, particularly in the Rocky Mountain region, who interface on a regular basis with people in the outdoors. Too numerous to name, you know who you are.

Abundant thanks go to Bruce Schwartz and Kirk Bol for vital statistics, interpretive consultant Alan Leftridge, Dr. Daniel Pletscher (University of Montana) for Rocky Mountain wolf information, and Drs. Paula Cushing, Dave Richman and Sandy Brantle for arachnid expertise.

Thanks to Gerri and Gordon Slabaugh of Adventure Publications for having faith in me and for really paying attention to my suggestions. That means a lot. Monica Ahlman and Brett Ortler at Adventure also made this project fun and easy to work on.

A day doesn't pass when I feel such gratitude to being married to the best editor, supporter, business partner, coach and playmate in the whole world! Thanks, Nancy, you are such a gift to me.

Finally, this book would not have been possible if there had not been a wonderful host of critters that love the taste of me. Imagine a world without things that bite! Wait . . . without them we would likely be dead. Hail the complex web of biological diversity!

Edited by Brett Ortler

Cover and book design by Jonathan Norberg
Cartoon illustrations by Erik Ahlman and Brenna Slabaugh
All chapter introduction artwork by Julie Martinez

See page 159 for photo credits by photographer and page number.

Table of Contents

Aware, Not Afraid

The last word in ignorance is the man who says of an animal or plant:
"What good is it?" If the land mechanism as a whole is good, then every part is
good, whether we understand it or not. If the biota, in the course of eons, has
built something we like but do not understand, then who but a fool would discard
seemingly useless parts? To keep every cog and wheel is the first precaution of
intelligent tinkering. —Aldo Leopold

Our nature, as humans, is to play favorites. Things that inflict pain tend to be "bad." Conversely, those species that we depend on for food or that provide us with recreational opportunities (such as hunting and fishing) are labeled as "good." We are categorical by nature. Humans are the only species that judge the "goodness" or "badness" of other creatures.

I want to challenge the reader to marvel in the adaptations of the biters and stingers in this book. Each has a unique set of adaptations, genius in design and function, and each plays an important role that benefits the whole system—including us. We should stand in wonder and awe of these beasts, and in so doing, come to know them and their places better.

The more we learn about something, the more we understand and respect it. It is doubtful that if you kill any of the stingers and biters in this book, you will significantly impact their population. However, remember that you have a choice, and they are not biting because they are "bad."

Each of us harbors fears. Research verifies that children learn many of their fears from adults, particularly their parents. A toddler who watches his parents cringe or overreact when a wasp flies near him, or when a spider or snake suddenly appears, will learn that such a response is normal. Children are not used to seeing their parents cringe in fear. This becomes an emotional bookmark in the child's life and is not easily forgotten. One of the best gifts you can give your child is to demonstrate curiosity and enthusiasm about the oddities (and yes, even the outcasts) of the animal world. This is a perfect opportunity to teach children respect, not fear.

It is important to note that a few critters bite or sting as part of their strategy for obtaining food, but many species will bite or sting only if they feel threatened or are mishandled. For many of the creatures covered in this book, the customary way to deal with them is to quickly kill them. Besides the obvious ethical issues involved with this approach, some of the critters in this book (such as the grizzly bear) are illegal to kill. Others, such as raccoons and black bears, have seasons regulating when they can be harvested.

It is my hope that the reader will look past the potentially troublesome aspects of these creatures and recognize how beneficial these biters and stingers are. Not only will I introduce the reader to the basic natural history of the animal, but I will give advice on how to avoid conflicts and, if necessary, how to treat a bite or sting.

This book is intended as a guide to animal species that might make an outing uncomfortable or painful, and can accompany a trip to a state park, a picnic, a day on the trout stream, camping, canoeing or backpacking. It can make your fishing expedition, backyard picnic or party more comfortable.

I used my own judgment to determine which species to include in this book. As a naturalist, I am an educator and nature is often my classroom. I have had the

good fortune of leading groups on various eco-trips throughout North America and into South America. Each area has its own unique assemblage of creatures. This book deals with species found in the Rocky Mountain region. Specifically, I have attempted to address the fauna found in northern New Mexico, eastern Utah, Idaho, Colorado, Wyoming and Montana.

In the United States, the Rocky Mountains extend from the

Canadian border in northern Montana all the way south to the Sangre de Cristo Mountains in New Mexico, a distance greater than 1,250 miles. The Rocky Mountain region is very biologically diverse and encompasses an expansive range of ecosystems, including everything from deserts to alpine meadows. These habitats host a variety of wildlife, too many species to include in this book. So I owe a special thanks to the naturalists, federal and state park personnel, and outdoor recreationists who provided me with lists of critters that most commonly bother or concern them and—more importantly—the public, at their respective centers or parks. This book, and particularly the list of biters and stingers, would not have been possible without their input.

While I respect that many people are wary of many species in this book, I can assure you, it is highly unlikely you will ever be injured by a wolf, bear, cougar, coyote, skunk or bat. Such species were added to this guide primarily to dispel myths and unfounded fears about them.

Contrary to popular belief, the most deadly creatures in the Rocky Mountain region are bees and wasps. Approximately 50 people die each year in the United States from allergic reactions to bee, wasp or hornet stings, while an average of 1 person is killed annually by an attack of a large wild mammal.

yellow jacket

To put things in perspective, I visited with an emergency room physician to ask about animal bites and stings. I asked, "Of all the bites and stings you deal with, which give you the greatest concern?" Almost immediately he responded, "Humans."

"Certainly, " he added, "we sometimes have to deal with disfiguring dog bites, but the ones that invariably lead to nasty infections are those delivered by humans." It turns out that legions of nasty anaerobic bacteria thrive between our teeth. Each of us can tolerate our own community of bacteria but not someone else's.

Of all four-legged beasts in the United States, the domestic dog—"man's best friend"—is responsible for many more bites (and deaths) than any wild animal. In 2008 alone, 33 human deaths were caused by dog bites, and over 1,000 patients were admitted to emergency rooms daily because of dog bites.

Another reality check is the fact that we attack and kill other humans at least 90,000 times more than bears attack us.

My hope is that this book will encourage you to explore the outdoors armed with a little more knowledge and with tips to make your experience more comfortable and pleasant. To get a better appreciation of the natural world and its role in our lives, we absolutely need the intimate connection of getting out there.

Enjoy the outdoors, and be aware—not afraid!

— Tom

Anaphylactic Shock, Rabies and a Dose of Reality

The majority of the time, the most pain you will feel from a bite or a sting will likely be temporary. The likelihood of being bitten by a rabid mammal or experiencing a severe allergic reaction to a sting is small. However, you need to be observant and aware of the biter/stinger. The following information is intended to educate the reader about anaphylactic shock and rabies.

Anaphylaxis is a serious allergic reaction resulting from an insect sting, a bug bite or from exposure to food or drug allergens. Anaphylactic shock is the condition that can result from anaphylaxis, if left untreated. Rabies is a life-threatening virus that attacks the central nervous system.

Having some background and knowledge of these two uncommon afflictions will make your outdoor experience more comfortable. The irony is that it's more likely that you'll be injured when traveling by automobile than to come down with either rabies or anaphylactic shock. Keep things in perspective.

ANAPHYLAXIS

Development of the following signs and symptoms within minutes of exposure to a bite or sting is a strong indication of anaphylaxis:

- Constriction of the airways that results in difficulty breathing
- Shock associated with a severe decrease in blood pressure
- Weak and rapid pulse
- Confusion or anxiety
- Dizziness or fainting
- Hives and itching
- Flushed or pale skin
- Nausea, vomiting or diarrhea

If you've had anaphylaxis or have a history of allergies or asthma, you may have a greater chance of having an anaphylactic reaction. Ask your doctor about obtaining an Anaphylaxis Emergency Treatment Kit or an EpiPen. Both contain injectable adrenaline (epinephrine) for allergic reactions.

RABIES

Rabies is a viral disease that invades the central nervous system of mammals, including humans. The virus is commonly transmitted in saliva, when an infected animal bites another animal or person.

- The origin of the word "rabies" comes from the Latin word *rabere,* which means "to rave or rage."

- Globally, more than 55,000 people die of rabies each year. Dogs are responsible for 99 percent of those deaths. Fortunately, few rabies deaths occur in the United States due to successful pet vaccination efforts.

- In the Rocky Mountain region, rabies is most commonly found in bats, followed by skunks. It also shows up in other mammals such as raccoons, foxes, coyotes, bobcats and domestic cats and dogs. There have even been isolated cases in livestock.

- Most recent cases of rabies in humans in the United States have occurred after the victim was bitten by an infected bat. (Reality check: It is estimated that less than 1 percent of bats carry rabies.) However, bats are rarely the cause of a rabies outbreak. They generally transmit the virus to other bats.

- In most areas where rabies outbreaks occur, the virus strain is traced back to dogs, cats, raccoons, skunks or other animals.

- After receiving an infectious bite, it takes anywhere from 20 to 60 days for the virus to reach your brain. Early symptoms might be subtle. These could include headache, sore throat, fatigue or fever.

- Treatment for rabies is no longer the horror story we used to hear about. You know, multiple shots in your belly. You will initially receive a shot of human rabies immune globulin (HRIG) near the site of the bite. The following series of 5 vaccination shots will be in the upper arm.

- If you are bitten by an animal and are unable to have the biting animal tested for rabies, you absolutely need to receive the rabies shots.

- Untreated, the rabies virus is fatal 100 percent of the time!

- The best prevention is to not handle or touch wild mammals. Don't be tempted to help a sick-looking animal. Seek out help from properly trained wildlife professionals.

No-see-ums

Despite their small size, these little gnats can drive people crazy and to the nearest shelter. I have known folks to pack up their tents, hook up their trailers and leave spectacular campgrounds to avoid a major hatch of no-see-ums.

No-see-ums can inflict misery simply due to their sheer numbers. Sometimes swarms are so thick that they are easily taken into our mouths, nose, ears and eyes.

About No-see-ums

These little insects fall into a group known as biting midges, also called "punkies" and no-see-ums. There are over 100 species in North America. When these little flying insurgents are bad, they can be worse than mosquitoes since they can easily infiltrate the average window screen.

Life and Times . . .

Like other flies, these tiny biters go through a complete metamorphosis. They go from egg to larva to pupa before finally reaching adulthood. This metamorphosis can take 2–6 weeks.

After ingesting a blood meal, the female seeks the edge of a wetland, where she lays her eggs on moist soil or mud. Some species can produce up to 450 eggs per batch. Eggs generally hatch within 2–10 days. The adult female only lives a few weeks.

The tiny, legless aquatic larvae scavenge on decaying organic matter in mud, sand, tree holes, water and vegetation. Species found in the Rocky Mountain region spend the winter in a dormant state in their larval stage and pupate in the spring before "emerging" as adults.

Males usually emerge first and are ready to mate when the females take wing. Mating usually occurs in flight, when receptive females fly into swarms of cooperative males.

Fascinating Facts

- No-see-ums belong to the order of true flies, or Diptera, which translates to "two" (Di) "wings" (ptera). There are more than 3,500 Diptera species in North America.

- While there are currently no issues with no-see-ums transmitting diseases to humans in the Rocky Mountain region, they are blamed for spreading bluetongue (a serious disease in ruminants such as sheep and cattle) among livestock in parts of the United States.

Thanks to No-see-ums

- No-see-ums are very important in the food chain, as many species of insects and fish feed on the larvae, pupae and adult insects.

- These tiny insects, particularly the nectar-seeking males, are important plant pollinators.

Myth Busters

MYTH: The female no-see-um dies after 1 egg-laying episode.

While this is true for some species, some females lay a second batch of eggs.

Why They Bite

Male no-see-ums do not bite. But the female needs a protein-rich blood meal in order to produce her eggs. She obtains it by biting a variety of involuntary donors such as reptiles, amphibians, birds and mammals—including humans.

Remarkably, some species of no-see-ums prey upon other insects, ingesting hemolymph, the equivalent of insect blood.

How They Bite

Like other biting flies, the female no-see-um has a tiny set of sharp mandibles, or jaws, that are used to cut into flesh. A natural blood thinner in her saliva makes it easier for her to suck up blood and helps to quickly secure a meal.

In itself, the nonvenomous bite is not exceedingly painful. However, after the injury has been dealt, the itching and discomfort can be miserable.

How Afraid Should I Be?

Other than temporary discomfort, there is little reason to worry. Small raised red welts and blisters can form and last for several days. The greatest concern is that sometimes an allergic reaction can occur. Such a reaction will usually show up resembling a skin rash or infection.

Preventing No-See-Um Bites

- The simplest protection to prevent bites is to wear protective clothing (long pants and long-sleeved shirts).

- Insect repellents containing DEET (N,N-diethyl-meta-toluamide) help reduce the likelihood of bites.

- Since their small size allows them to crawl through the conventional 16-mesh wire window screen, a finer mesh might be required to keep them outdoors.

- These tiny flies are weak fliers, so indoor fans at high speeds can be used to keep the insects out of small areas.

- Some people have good luck with a spray-on sunscreen (SPF 30). Although it is DEET-free, it is recommended that you shower it off each night.

THINK TWICE

Think twice about where you want to hike, picnic or camp. No-see-ums tend to stay in the vicinity of their wetland breeding grounds. Avoid these areas, particularly at dawn and dusk, when these insects are most active.

Think twice about leaving your porch light on. No-see-ums are attracted to lights.

Treatment of Bites

- Clean the bites with soap and water.

- Itching and swelling can be reduced with the help of anti-itch and anti-inflammatory lotions and creams.

- Aspirin or Tylenol might offer additional relief. Do not administer aspirin to children under 15 years old.

- If blisters occur, apply an antibacterial/antibiotic ointment and keep the blisters loosely covered to allow air passage to help dry them out.

BOTTOM LINE

Protective clothing and other simple precautions will keep most no-see-ums at bay. But other than a little temporary discomfort, there is no reason to fear them. Their bite is neither venomous nor very painful. And although the itching and welts can be miserable, the discomfort is typically short-lived.

Chiggers

There is something so inviting about pausing along the lush grassy edge of a stream, a pond or a lake. These are popular places to picnic, nap or sunbathe, but such episodes of relaxation can turn miserable if there are chiggers lurking nearby. Unbeknownst to you, these tiny, stealthy mites can make their way onto your body where they delicately probe your skin. As their bite is imperceptible, you will likely learn that chiggers were present in the area after the fact—when you go to bed and the itching begins. Woe to the person who begins scratching! It only makes it worse.

About Chiggers

Like ticks and spiders, chiggers are arachnids, not insects. Chiggers start out very small; their larvae are only $1/150$ of an inch in diameter, and it's actually these tiny larvae that cause us discomfort.

As chiggers develop, they grow larger and their diet changes. As nymphs and adults, chiggers no longer feed upon us; they prey upon insect eggs and small invertebrates in the soil.

Chiggers are found only in the southern parts of the Rocky Mountain region, occasionally in parts of Colorado and New Mexico. They are sometimes called mites or red bugs because adults are covered in dense, red hairs.

Life and Times . . .

Like other arachnids, chiggers go through 4 life stages: egg, larva, nymph and adult. The complete life cycle takes roughly 50–70 days.

Adult male chiggers die shortly after mating. Fertilized females lay up to 400 eggs in early spring after the soil begins to warm. The female chigger dies shortly after laying her eggs.

In a matter of days, the eggs hatch, producing the chigger's tiny larval stage, which is barely visible to the naked eye. Shortly after hatching, the six-legged larvae climb to a perch, where they can easily latch onto a passing host. Unlike their tick cousins, who sit and wait, chigger larvae are nearly constantly on the move. Larvae feed on a number of host species, including mammals, birds, reptiles and even some amphibians.

Larvae are most likely to be found in areas with thick vegetation and high humidity. Due to their thin skin and small size, these unusual animals are susceptible to dehydration. Sandy, dry areas are not humid enough for their survival.

After 3 days of feeding on the host, the larva drops off and crawls into the soil, where it develops into the nymph stage. Nymphs are essentially scaled-down versions of adults and feed on tiny soil invertebrates until they are ready to change into adults. Both nymphs and adults have 8 legs.

Three generations of chiggers are born over the course of spring, summer and early fall.

Fascinating Facts

- A larval chigger's saliva includes an enzyme that turns skin cells into a liquid, which the larva then drinks.

- Like mosquitoes, chiggers are attracted to the carbon dioxide given off by a passing host.

- Chiggers are capable of getting all over a person's body in minutes. The climb from a victim's shoe to the belt line (a favorite point of attack) is an ascent that takes about 15 minutes. That's no small feat for such a small creature; when climbing on a human host, a chigger covers a distance equal to 5,000 times its total length. That's akin to a human climbing a tall mountain on an empty stomach!

Thanks to Chiggers

- A chigger's favorite foods include eggs of springtails (tiny soil insects), isopods (terrestrial crustaceans such as wood lice) and even pesky mosquitoes!

- Chiggers, like other parasites, are a sign of a healthy and diverse natural world.

Myth Busters

MYTH: Itching is caused by chiggers that burrow under your skin and die.

Chiggers never burrow under skin, and they don't die on their host. Only their delicate mouthparts pierce the skin; the small dot visible inside the welt is called the stylostome and is the tube where the chigger feeds. The female jigger, or chigoe flea, does literally attach by burrowing under skin to lay its eggs.

MYTH: Chiggers get their red color from feeding on blood.

Actually, chiggers are born red. Chiggers feed on liquefied skin tissue, not blood. After a full meal, a chigger turns yellow.

MYTH: Nail polish applied to chigger welts helps relieve the itch.

This myth persists because of the belief that the nail polish will smother the chigger, preventing it from inflicting more pain. Nevertheless, the stylostome, not the chigger, causes the itching. In fact, if you have a chigger welt, then it's probably too late; the chigger has already fed and is long gone.

Why They Bite

Remember, chiggers only bite as youngsters, during their larval stage of development. In order to develop properly they must feed on the skin tissue of a host. Later in life, they feed on insects and vegetation in the soil.

How They Bite

Like ticks, chiggers insert microscopic beak-like mouthparts into skin depressions in the host. These piercing mouthparts are delicate and can only penetrate thin skin, such as skin follicles, or areas where skin wrinkles and folds. That's why most chigger bites occur around the ankles, the armpits, the back of the knees and below the belt line.

At least 1 hour, and more likely 2–3 hours, pass before the chigger actually starts feeding. The chigger releases enzymes that liquefy the skin, and the body reacts by hardening the cells on all sides of the saliva route. Eventually a hard tubelike structure called a stylostome is formed.

THINK TWICE

Think twice about sitting down for a rest or picnic in thick grassy or brushy areas.

Think twice about aggressively scratching any chigger bites. Your scratching can lead to a secondary infection.

This pipelike structure contains the digesting saliva; the chigger inserts its delicate mouthparts into the stylostome and sucks up the liquid skin tissue. In this way, the stylostome serves as something like a tall drinking glass.

If a chigger feeds undisturbed, the stylostome and surrounding tissue become inflamed, creating an itchy red welt. The longer the chigger feeds, the deeper the stylostome grows, and the larger the welt becomes.

If undisturbed, the chigger remains on the host for 3–4 days. Though you might detect the first bites in a matter of 3–4 hours, the worst itching generally occurs 24–48 hours after the first bites.

How Afraid Should I Be?

There is no need to be overly afraid of chigger bites. Though the itching can be agonizing and persistent for a couple of days, chigger bites don't cause any human diseases or long-term disabilities. With that said, try not to scratch chigger bites; vigorous scratching can lead to secondary infections.

Preventing Chigger Bites

- Avoiding chiggers is the best prevention, so it's important to choose the right clothing on your outings in chigger country. Lightly colored, tightly knit clothing offers better protection from wandering chiggers and keeps you cooler. Tightly woven socks, long sleeves and long pants are a good choice, and it's best to tuck your pants into your boots or shoes. Be sure to button collars to close off additional access points. *Do not* wear shorts, sleeveless shirts, sandals or any clothing that gives chiggers easy access to your skin.

- Mosquito repellents can help prevent chigger bites. Apply repellent to exposed skin and around openings in clothes, such as cuffs, waistbands, shirtfronts and boot tops, as this forces chiggers to cross the treated line to get inside your clothes. It's important to apply repellent often, as it only remains potent for short periods.

- Powdered sulfur, which is also known as sublimed sulfur, is an excellent deterrent against chiggers when applied around openings in clothing. It is available at most pharmacies. If you are in a heavily infested area, rub the powdered sulfur over the skin on your arms, legs and waist. Some outdoor enthusiasts rub on a mixture of half talcum powder and half sulfur powder. Before using powdered sulfur, be aware that sulfur has a strong, rotten egg-like odor, and it is a skin irritant for some people. Experiment on a small skin area the first time you try it.

- While outside, avoid tall grasses and brush. If you're going to sit down on something, choose a rock that has been heated by the sun. Chiggers avoid objects that are hotter than 99 °F. (Temperatures below 42 °F will kill them.)

- After an outing outdoors, change clothes as soon as possible, and wash them before wearing them again. If you don't, the chiggers will simply get to you next time you put them on.

- To avoid encounters closer to home and keep chiggers out of your yard, remove their preferred habitat by clearing brush and weeds and keeping the grass short. Chiggers don't do well in areas that are well groomed.

Treatment of Bites

- The best treatment for chigger bites is a warm and soapy bath. Vigorous scrubbing will remove any attached and feeding chiggers before the itching begins. If bathing is not an option, chiggers can be removed by thoroughly rubbing bare skin down with a towel or cloth.

- If chigger bites develop, itching can persist for 2 weeks. Over-the-counter local anesthetic creams, such as benzocaine and camphor-phenol, can provide some relief. Other treatment options include topical corticosteroids, oral antihistamines, and soothing compresses such as Domeboro or Aveeno. Rarely, some people are allergic to chigger bites and require prescription medications.

- Some home remedies are popular; many people swear that itching subsides if you apply a paste of meat tenderizer (salt-free papain) or baking soda on the welts. Another popular home remedy for itching relief is to sponge vinegar on welts.

- Some home remedies for chigger bites involve household chemicals. These "treatments" often include dangerous chemicals such as kerosene, turpentine, ammonia, alcohol, gasoline, salt or dry-cleaning fluid. Such chemicals can be harmful and the treatments don't work, so don't try them.

- Don't scratch chigger bites too vigorously, as this can lead to a nasty secondary bacterial infection. If you do scratch, disinfect the chigger bite with topical antiseptics.

- Eventually your body will break down the cause of your itch—the feeding tube of the chigger. Patience is a good virtue in dealing with chigger bites.

BOTTOM LINE

You can avoid chigger bites by wearing the proper clothing, watching where you sit or walk, and by taking precautions after venturing outdoors. If you develop welts from chigger bites, you can find comfort in knowing that the itching will be gone in a couple of weeks.

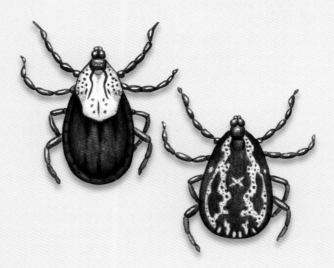

Ticks

Casually ask someone, "Is that a tick on your arm?" and you will likely witness an immediate and urgent response. For such a little fellow—no bigger than one of these typed letters—the tick easily prompts even the most macho of men to take defensive action. And even after the hitchhiking tick is pointed out, there is the predictable, contagious outbreak of twitching and scratching among people nearby.

Such is the power of this little creature.

(above left: female dog or wood tick; above right: male dog or wood tick)

About Ticks

Ticks are not insects. Like spiders, mites and scorpions, they are arachnids. Adult ticks have 8 legs, while the larvae have 6 legs.

dog or wood tick   black-legged or deer tick   Rocky Mountain wood tick

Of the more than 30 tick species that live in the Rocky Mountain region, the Rocky Mountain wood tick and the American dog tick are the species most associated with humans. The western black-legged tick (also known as the deer tick) is also present, but it is found only on the western edge of the region in parts of Utah and Idaho.

The Rocky Mountain wood tick is about ¹/₈ of an inch in length and slightly larger after it ingests a blood meal. These brown ticks turn gray when engorged. The female has a gray-colored disk behind her head, while the male's disk is mottled brown and gray.

Like the Rocky Mountain wood tick, the American dog tick is also referred to as a wood tick; it is the larger of the two, approximately ¼ inch in length. The female has a cream-colored disk behind her head, while the male lacks the disk and has 2 thin, lighter-colored stripes running down his back. This tick is the primary carrier of Rocky Mountain spotted fever.

Unlike wood ticks, black-legged ticks have no white or cream-colored markings on their backs. They are smaller (about ¹/₈ inch long), dark brown to black and teardrop shaped. Females usually have an area behind their head that is orange to red in color. Black-legged ticks are the primary transmitter of Lyme disease.

Life and Times . . .

Under ideal conditions, ticks have a 2-year life cycle that includes blood-feeding stages as larvae, nymphs and adults. In the spring, tick eggs hatch and tiny larval ticks emerge. Sometimes referred to as seed ticks, they typically feed on the blood of small rodents such as mice. After developing into nymphs, they feed on small to medium-sized mammals such as chipmunks. Adults seek out larger animals, including white-tailed deer. Because female black-legged ticks secure blood meals from deer for egg production, deer play a key role in maintaining high tick populations.

In the Rocky Mountain region, humans are most at risk from May to September, when ticks are in the nymph stage. However, adult ticks can bite, so caution is advised from April through December.

Fascinating Facts

- Ticks have been reported to feed on at least 125 different kinds of animals, including 57 bird varieties, 54 mammal species and 14 types of lizards.

- The folds in a tick's skin allows it to greatly expand in size. An engorged female tick might increase her weight by 200 times!

Thanks to Ticks

- Ticks are prey for many species of birds and an important part of the food chain.

Myth Busters

MYTH: Ticks will leap out of trees onto you!

Ticks are crawlers, not jumpers. Leaping insects, such as crickets or grass-hoppers, have longer, larger legs. A tick's legs are better suited for climbing up to ambush sites, where they lie in wait for a possible host to pass by.

Why They Bite

Simply put, ticks bite only to secure a meal. They require blood meals to change from one life stage to the next. An adult female also requires a blood meal to produce her thousands of eggs.

How They Bite

An electron microscope image of a tick's mouthparts is reminiscent of the aliens portrayed in the *Star Wars* movies. Creepy!

The tick's beak-like mouthparts have backward-pointing barbs that allow the tick to remain anchored for a successful bloodletting. After attachment, the tick secretes a protein-rich cementing substance that helps keep itself in place.

electron microscope image of black-legged or deer tick mouthparts

This patch of cement, which resembles a small chunk of your skin, can often be seen when a tick is removed. As the tick feeds, it releases saliva that contains special compounds that thin the blood and suppress pain.

How Afraid Should I Be?

Tick bites can cause some discomfort, such as itching or a rash, but alone they are not a major threat. However, in the past 25 years, ticks have become more of a concern as they have been found to carry serious diseases.

So let's look at a few of the tick-borne diseases and where they are usually found. In the Rocky Mountain region there are 6 tick-borne illnesses that are most commonly reported: Colorado tick fever, Rocky Mountain spotted fever, tick-borne relapsing fever, Lyme disease, tick paralysis and tularemia.

black-legged or deer tick

COLORADO TICK FEVER

Colorado tick fever is the most common tick-borne disease throughout the Rocky Mountain region. The Rocky Mountain wood tick is the primary vector in transmitting this disease to humans. In Colorado there are roughly 200 cases reported each year, but it is likely that many cases go unreported.

The disease is a result of a viral infection caused by the bite of an infected wood tick. The tick acquires the virus after feeding on the blood of small mammals, such as ground squirrels, tree squirrels and chipmunks, particularly those that reside at elevations above 5,000 feet.

The infection occurs most often in spring and early summer. Symptoms are flu-like and generally last 1–3 days. Symptoms are similar to other tick-borne diseases, and include chills, headaches, nausea, muscle aches and fatigue. Generally, the disease resolves on its own and disappears.

ROCKY MOUNTAIN SPOTTED FEVER

Rocky Mountain spotted fever (RMSF) is another tick-borne disease found in the region, but it is rare here, despite its name. Transmitted primarily by the American dog tick, and sometimes by the Rocky Mountain wood tick, the most common symptom for this disease is a small spotted rash that occurs first on the palms of the hands or the soles of the feet, and then spreads to other parts of the body. Muscle pain and fever are additional common symptoms. Even though it is easily treatable, RMSF is often misdiagnosed because people don't think about the disease being in that area.

engorged dog or wood tick

TICK-BORNE RELAPSING FEVER

Tick-borne relapsing fever (TBRF) is an infection caused by a bacterium found in ticks that feed on rodents. TBRF can only be spread if an infected tick bites you. The disease is very rare in this region.

Symptoms may include a sudden fever, chills, headaches, muscle or joint aches, nausea, and a rash may also occur. These symptoms continue for 2–9 days and then disappear. This cycle may continue for several weeks if the person is not treated with the appropriate antibiotics. Untreated, TBRF can cause serious complications.

LYME DISEASE

Most cases of Lyme disease occur outside the Rocky Mountain region, and while Lyme disease is extremely uncommon in the area, it's a serious disease that merits attention.

Lyme disease is caused by a bacterium called a spirochete (spy-row-keet). Spirochetes can only be transmitted when a tick bites a host and remains attached for more than 48 hours. About 70–90 percent of patients infected with Lyme disease develop a circular, red "bull's-eye" rash at the site of the bite. Left untreated, Lyme disease can be serious, affecting the skin, joints, heart and nervous system. Thankfully, antibiotics are often effective; the earlier antibiotics are administered, the greater the likelihood of successful treatment.

THINK TWICE

Think twice before letting your dog or cat indoors without a good tick check after an outing in the woods or grasslands during tick season. Neglecting your pet might simply allow a host of uninvited ticks into your home.

The Centers for Disease Control (CDC) estimates that only 10–20 percent of Lyme disease cases are reported. Even so, over 30,000 new cases were diagnosed nationally last year and the rate of infection is increasing.

TICK PARALYSIS

Tick paralysis is a disease that sometimes occurs when ticks—most commonly the Rocky Mountain wood tick—remain attached to a person for an extended period. Caused by a neurotoxin in the tick's saliva, symptoms include difficulty walking, numbness in the legs and arms and difficulty in breathing. A doctor should always address breathing difficulties. Children are most susceptible to tick paralysis and may also display flu-like symptoms. The paralysis starts lower in the body and moves its way up. Fortunately, once the tick is removed, the condition is reversible and recovery is rapid.

dog or wood tick

TULAREMIA

Tularemia, also known as rabbit fever, is an infectious disease caused by a bacterium usually associated with rabbits and hares, but it is sometimes present in other small mammals. Humans can acquire the bacterium when bitten by an infected tick, after handling infected animal carcasses, or by ingesting the bacterium in contaminated food or water. Most people acquire the illness from a tick, an insect bite or after coming into contact with the blood of infected animals. It is not communicable.

Tularemia symptoms vary depending on how the bacterium is acquired, and can include fever, chills, headaches, muscle aches, joint pain, dry cough, progressive weakness and pneumonia (if the bacterium is inhaled). If contaminated blood comes into contact with skin, symptoms can include ulcers on the skin. If infected meat is ingested, symptoms could include a sore throat, upset stomach, diarrhea and vomiting.

Preventing Tick Bites

- Prevent ticks from getting to your skin by wearing appropriate clothing, such as long pants with the cuffs tucked into shin-high socks or boots. Light-colored clothing makes it easier to spot a hitchhiking tick.

- Limit your time in tall grass and brushy areas, particularly in the spring and fall.

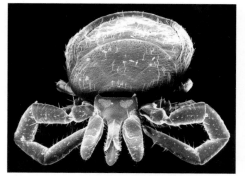

- Chemical warfare on ticks can help. A 0.5 percent concentration of permethrin sprayed on your pants and shirt can be very effective. Note it is important that you don't spray permethrin on your skin. Some folks claim that spraying a mosquito repellent with a high concentration of DEET on their clothes also repels ticks.

electron microscope image of black-legged or deer tick

- Perform diligent tick checks after outings. If appropriate, ask for help in checking hard-to-see spots, such as your back.

So you find a fastened tick. Now what?

- Simply put, the longer a tick feeds on you, the greater the odds of it transmitting a tick-borne illness such as Lyme disease. Immediate tick removal lessens the risk of infection.

- To properly remove a tick, it is best to grasp it with a fine tweezers, but fingers will do the job. Do not use petroleum jelly, gasoline, nail polish remover or a hot match.

- Grasp the tick as close to the point of attachment as possible and pull straight up, gently but firmly. Do not jerk or twist the tick, and don't squeeze it, since that might push infectious substances into the wound.

- Don't worry if the tick's mouthparts remain in the skin. Your body will reject the foreign material and be rid of it in a few days. The bite might become reddish and even warm to the touch, but that's a normal reaction.

- After the tick is removed, disinfect the skin thoroughly and wash your hands with soap and water.

- While it might be difficult to determine how long the tick has been fastened, it will help if you recall a situation when you might have picked up a tick, such as a hike in the woods, camping or petting a dog that had recently been outdoors. This information will be particularly helpful should you later require medical treatment.

Treatment of Bites

- Watch the bite site for a possible secondary infection or infectious rash for up to 30 days. If you experience persistent headaches or fever within 3–4 days after a tick bite is discovered, it's a good idea to get it checked out.

- If you find an engorged tick in your home, it has already fed. If you don't have pets, the tick likely fed on you or family members, so consult a doctor to be on the safe side. Your best defense is to watch for ticks and to stay up-to-date about tick-borne diseases.

BOTTOM LINE

Tick bites can cause mild discomfort, itching or a rash but are not a major threat to human health. Although tick-borne diseases such as Lyme disease are a concern, an infected tick must be attached for more than 48 hours to transmit disease. Preventative measures and frequent tick checks can greatly reduce your risk.

Black Flies

I recall a particularly memorable day of fishing brook trout in northern Minnesota when I had plenty of company on the water. Even though I finished the trip early so I could attend an evening wedding, I wore 42 black fly welts to the marriage ceremony. Yes, I really counted them.

A popular fishing fly, "the black gnat," is named after this bloodthirsty insect. Perhaps there is some sort of justice that this fly can be successfully used to catch "trout that bite!"

About Black Flies

Of the approximately 150 species of black flies in North America, some are fierce biters. Other nonbiting black flies are simply a nuisance as they swarm around your face.

It hardly seems fair that such a small creature can cause so much misery. Stealthier than a mosquito's high-pitched whine, black flies swoop in for a meal of blood without even pricking us. They have tiny mandibles and in essence cut into our exposed flesh.

Life and Times . . .

Like mosquitoes, deer flies and horse flies, black flies begin life underwater. Female black flies lay their tiny cream-colored eggs at sunset on the water's surface or on wet vegetation along the shoreline. Each lays 200–800 eggs, which become attached to stones, sticks or vegetation in shallow, fast-running creeks, streams and rivers.

After hatching, the black or brown-colored larvae anchor themselves to rocks, sunken branches and other underwater objects. They filter microscopic food particles with their fine brushlike mouthparts as the current flows by them. The larvae are sometimes so abundant and concentrated that they look like underwater moss. This stage lasts 6–7 months (usually over the winter).

The pupa is covered by a silken cocoon that is attached to underwater objects with small hooklike appendages; the pupa uses silk "rope" and loops to move, almost like an underwater mountaineer. The cocoons look like slipper-shaped silken cases, and they are attached to the bottom by the "toe" of the slipper, with the opening floating downstream.

When the fly emerges from the stream, it immediately flies to nearby vegetation, where its body hardens. (Unlike us, insects have an exoskeleton—a skeleton on the outside of their body.) Even after the flies emerge from the stream, the empty "slipper" cocoons can be seen underwater.

After emerging, most black flies live 2–3 weeks, though some long-lived varieties survive up to 85 days.

Fascinating Facts

- Only female black flies bite.

- After pupating in the stream, an emerging black fly rides to the surface in a tiny bubble of air.

- Amazingly, hordes of black flies all hatch in the same time period.

- Their sheer numbers make them a threat to livestock, poultry, wildlife and humans. In the far north of the region, the black fly hatch often contributes to the movements of caribou and impacts the survival of caribou calves (fawns).

Thanks to Black Flies

- The aquatic larvae provide a food source for many fish species, including trout.

- Birds and insects, such as dragonflies, feed on adult black flies.

- The male black fly feeds on flower nectar and is an important plant pollinator.

Myth Busters

MYTH: Large swarms of black flies swirling along a river or stream are very dangerous.

Though they look intimidating, these swarms are made up of nonbiting males. The female, when ready to mate, flies into the swarm to find a willing male.

Why They Bite

Like their bloodletting mosquito neighbor, it is only the female black fly that must get a blood meal to assure the next generation. But unlike mosquitoes, which are most active at twilight and night, black flies are daytime biters and prefer low wind conditions. Luckily, in the Rocky Mountain region, black flies are only a nuisance for about 3 weeks, primarily in late May and June.

How They Bite

The female's bite cuts a small hole, which quickly wells up with blood, and she feeds on this blood. Her saliva contains anticoagulants—blood thinners—which make it easier to feed. These blood thinners are also the reason that the bite continues to bleed after she leaves, and are believed to cause allergic reactions. It's another case where, as with the mosquito, insect "spit" can make for an uncomfortable outing.

black fly

How Afraid Should I Be?

The bite first appears as a small red spot that might become slightly swollen. It then becomes itchy, irritating and more swollen. This reaction can last several days.

With multiple bites, itching is sometimes accompanied by an allergic reaction. Though not life-threatening, it can cause mild to severe symptoms in sensitive individuals. A strong reaction might produce fever, nausea and allergic dermatitis.

Children are particularly vulnerable to black flies and may experience far more bites than adults who are outdoors in the same area.

Black flies also are known for attacking poultry and livestock. Since these flies are most pesky during the daytime, some folks will keep their poultry and livestock indoors during intense fly outbreaks in early summer.

Preventing Black Fly Bites

PHYSICAL BARRIERS

- The easiest way to avoid black fly bites is to avoid areas around swift-flowing streams during late May and June. However, that is unreasonable for most of us, since this is a lovely time to be outdoors.

- Since black flies are daytime feeders, scheduling outings for evenings and nighttime will lessen your contact with them.

- Avoid perfumes and colognes. Black flies are also attracted to perspiration.

- Don't wear dark-colored clothing. Wearing light-colored, loose-fitting clothing really does help.

- If flies are numerous, a head net or bug jacket is essential. These small insects are persistent and will squeeze through any opening in your clothes, including slight gaps at pant cuffs, the belt line and shirtsleeves.

CHEMICAL REPELLENTS

Bug repellents are not very effective on black flies. If you choose to use them, use those with DEET. However, some studies indicate that wearing DEET might actually attract more black flies.

THINK TWICE

Think twice before camping next to that beautiful rushing stream in early summer. It's a prime breeding ground for black flies.

Think twice about wearing your favorite dark blue windbreaker when hiking or camping in black fly country in early summer. Go with light-colored clothing instead.

OTHER TRICKS IN OUTWITTING BLACK FLIES

- Sew a strip of Velcro on the sleeve openings of long-sleeved shirts to seal out black flies.

- Use large rubber bands around your pant cuffs to close off entry to your legs. (I have also tucked my pants into the tops of my socks.)

Treatment of Bites

- Wash the bites with warm water and soap. Relieve itching with products such as Benadryl and anti-itching compounds and anti-inflammatory lotions and creams.

- If an allergic reaction occurs, seek immediate medical treatment.

BOTTOM LINE

A black fly's bite can produce a welt, but the reaction only lasts a few days. And despite their taste for blood, these little biters aren't all bad. At various life stages they provide food for fish, birds and dragonflies. Plus, the male is an important pollinator of many species of plants.

Mosquitoes

According to the Thompson River Indians of British Columbia, Thunder asked Mosquito why he was so fat, and Mosquito replied that he sucked on trees. He didn't want to admit that he really fed on people, because he didn't want Thunder to eat up all the people and deny him of his prey. Mosquito's plan worked very well, and his story explains why Thunder now shoots trees instead of people.

—*Legends of the Earth, Sea, and Sky: An Encyclopedia of Nature Myths* by Tamra Andrews

About Mosquitoes

Although the Rocky Mountain region is home to only 50 species of mosquitoes—a fraction the 2,500-plus species of mosquitoes found in the world—they are easily one of the most abundant biters you'll encounter outdoors. Taken alone, a single mosquito doesn't seem all that intimidating. But what the mosquito lacks in stature, it makes up in numbers and fearless tenacity. Swarms of droning mosquitoes have chased countless picnickers and campers indoors, and they've even driven wanted criminals out of hiding. Fortunately, there's no need to let them ruin your outdoor adventures.

Life and Times . . .

Mosquitoes (genus *Culex*) are members of the order Diptera. Considered true flies, they are related to houseflies and midges. Mosquitoes have 2 scaled wings, 6 long legs and, of course, a long, piercing proboscis (or beak).

Female mosquitoes lay 200–400 eggs in quiet marshes, swamps or ponds, and in other places that hold stagnant water, such as ditches, old tires and hoofprints. The eggs hatch within days. The tiny larva hangs upside down (like the letter "J") at the surface of the water. It feeds almost continuously on microscopic plant fragments.

About a dozen days later the larva changes (pupates) into the adult mosquito. The pupa begins to fill its pupal covering with air until the skin splits open and out emerges the wobbly adult mosquito. It stands, resting, on the surface of its watery home for about a half an hour before it flies to nearby grass or brush.

Fascinating Facts

- Only female mosquitoes bite.

- Male mosquitoes feed on rotting fruits or nectar from flowers.

- The female's wings beat 250–500 times per second; the male's feathery antennae help him pick up their species-specific frequency and pitch.

- Mosquitoes are capable of mating within 2 days of hatching. A female mosquito mates only once in her life. She will receive all the sperm needed to produce up to 400 eggs.

Thanks to Mosquitoes

- Mosquitoes are a main food source for other insects and wildlife such as ducklings and young fish. A single little brown bat may eat 5,000 mosquitoes in 1 night!

- Their larvae voraciously process tons of rotting plants (detritus) in wetlands.

- Mosquitoes are important plant pollinators in the Rocky Mountain region.

Myth Busters

MYTH: All mosquitoes are alike and can be controlled the same way.

There are more than 170 mosquito species in North America alone, and different species exhibit different behaviors. Some feed just before nightfall, while others feed around the clock or whenever a host is near. Timing is essential when targeting the winged adults, as chemical spraying is most effective when meteorological conditions, such as wind and humidity, are favorable.

MYTH: Bug zappers are effective against mosquitoes.

Researchers found that while ultraviolet or black light bug zappers do attract and kill thousands of insects within a 24-hour period, only 6.4 percent of a 5-day catch consists of mosquitoes. Of that, only half of the mosquitoes killed were the blood-feeding females. This is clearly not a good choice for controlling mosquitoes.

MYTH: The mosquito dies after she takes a blood meal.

Mosquitoes are capable of biting more than once. After the female mosquito takes a blood meal she completes the development of her eggs and may deposit up to 200 of them at a time. She may seek another blood meal and lay again.

Why They Bite

Mosquitoes require the proteins found in the blood of warm-blooded animals to produce eggs, which assure there will be future generations of mosquitoes. As the most numerous mammals on the planet, humans are a big part of the mosquito's dinner buffet.

How They Bite

The female mosquito uses sight to locate a warm-blooded host; females also can detect the host's body heat, as well as the carbon dioxide released during respiration. Once she finds a host, she pierces its skin and releases an anticoagulant (a blood thinner) into the host. Proteins found in the insect's saliva create the itch and welt after the mosquito bites.

How Afraid Should I Be?

Mosquito-borne diseases, such as malaria, are a serious threat in much of the world. Thankfully, in the Rocky Mountain region, mosquito bites are mostly just a painful irritation. With that said, residents should be aware of the recent arrival of West Nile Virus (WNV) in the region.

WEST NILE VIRUS

- Mosquitoes are the main vectors of WNV, which interferes with the central nervous system and causes inflammation of brain tissue. A mosquito may become infected with the virus by feeding on infected birds; if an infected mosquito bites a human or animal, the virus may be injected into the new host.

- Your risk of becoming seriously ill from WNV is very low. Even in areas where the virus is circulating, very few mosquitoes are infected. And fewer than 1 in 150 people who are bitten and become infected get severely ill. People over 50 years old and the chronically ill are at the highest risk of developing severe symptoms.

- Most people infected with WNV will not show symptoms. Others might experience mild symptoms such as fever, headache, nausea or vomiting and sometimes swollen lymph glands or a skin rash on the torso. Mild symptoms can last from a few days to several weeks. Severe symptoms include high fever, headache, stupor, coma, vision loss, numbness and paralysis. These symptoms might last for several weeks, and the effects could be permanent.

Preventing Mosquito Bites

PHYSICAL BARRIERS

The most effective means of dealing with mosquitoes is to put a barrier between yourself and the insect.

- Limit your time outdoors at dusk and dawn, when mosquitoes are most active.

- Wear loose-fitting, light-colored clothes that allow air movement but prevent the probing of mosquitoes. Dark clothing attracts mosquitoes.

- Head nets and bug jackets made of fine mesh keep insects from reaching your skin, yet allow air movement. Some are made to absorb repellents.

- Use screen tents to enclose picnic tables and lawn chairs.

NATURAL MOSQUITO REPELLENTS

- Oil of lemon eucalyptus repels mosquitoes. Citronella can work, too—but must be applied more often than synthetic chemicals. Some people claim success using Avon Skin-So-Soft, while others believe eating a clove of raw garlic each day will give their skin an odor that keeps mosquitoes away. (Their friends probably stay away, too!)

- Outdoor products, such as mosquito coils or citronella candles or torches, can create uncomfortable air space for mosquitoes.

CHEMICAL REPELLENTS

- The most common and effective repellent ingredient is DEET (N, N-diethyl-meta-toluamide). However, it can cause eye and sinus irritation, headaches, insomnia and confusion. Repellents with high DEET concentrations can melt some synthetic materials, dissolve paint and leave bad odors.

- Permethrin is a synthetic broad-spectrum insecticide. Your skin metabolizes, or breaks down, permethrin in less than 20 minutes after contact. When applied to clothing, it can last for hours.

OTHER TRICKS IN OUTWITTING MOSQUITOES

- When setting up your camp or picnic, choose a location with good airflow, away from thick underbrush and low areas.
- Learn to put up with them! Your body is amazingly adaptable and you will build up a natural resistance over time.

THINK TWICE

Synthetic repellents and insecticides are dangerous chemicals that are potentially harmful to you and the environment. Apply them with care and always read and follow the label instructions.

Treatment of Bites

- Soak a washcloth with cool water and press it on the bite(s).

- Products such as Benadryl and other anti-itch and anti-inflammatory medicines help relieve itching and swelling.

- The juice from an aloe vera plant can be rubbed on bites for relief.

- Apply a simple paste made of baking soda and water (use only enough water to form a sticky paste).

- Jewelweed or touch-me-not (*Impatiens biflora*) can help reduce itching. Pull up a plant from a site where it is abundant, squeeze its succulent stem and roots until it is juicy and rub the plant juices on the affected area.

BOTTOM LINE

Mosquitoes are one of the most abundant biters you will encounter outdoors. Fortunately, they are mostly just a painful irritation. Though West Nile Virus occurs in most of the Rocky Mountain region, your chances of being infected are remote.

Spiders

In E. B. White's classic tale ,*Charlotte's Web*, we are introduced to a sweet spider heroine, Charlotte. Even her charming manner and good web penmanship could not lift spiders out of their reputation of permanent Halloween status. Humans have maligned these amazing architects for eons.

Take a close look at a spider and it will mesmerize you with the engineering of its beautiful webs, its patience, stealth and sheer beauty. Who could resist the loving stare of 8 eyes?

About Spiders

There are currently more than 35,000 known species of spiders in the world, with thousands of additional species waiting to be classified. The U.S. is home to roughly 3,500 spider species, and roughly 1,000 species reside in the Rocky Mountain region. However, the greatest number of spider species are found in the southern part of the region, especially in northern New Mexico.

Only 1 group of spiders in this region—the widow spiders—are potentially dangerous, as they can deliver a seriously dangerous bite.

Life and Times . . .

Spiders, like insects, are invertebrates (they have no backbone). Unlike insects, they have 8 legs and 2 primary body parts: the cephalothorax (front body section) and the abdomen, which is larger. Like their tick, mite and scorpion cousins, spiders are arachnids.

All spiders are hunters. They either actively hunt or they hunt from a web. Spiderwebs are made of silk, and all species of spiders create silk. Spider silk isn't just for webs though; it's used in web building, in egg cases, to wrap up prey, to create retreat shelters and even for sperm storage when mating.

Male spiders are smaller than females and a male can often be recognized by his unique pair of pedipalps, or "palps." These palps resemble a pair of legs but more accurately resemble a pair of "feelers." They are located directly in front of the pair of legs closest to the spider's face. The tips of the male's palps are swollen, resembling a pair of boxing gloves. These serve as sperm receptacles for mating.

In some species, the male locates the female through the use of pheromones, chemicals spiders produce to affect the behavior or physiology of other members of their species. Among some species, males recognize the silk draglines of a female. After a cautious courtship, mating will occur. If the male's timing is off, the female might eat him!

Among most species, females generally lay their eggs in the summer, a week or so after mating. All of the eggs hatch simultaneously, and the hundreds of young are born blind. After a few days, the young can see and move. For several days, they subsist on an internal egg yolk. As they mature, they learn that their brothers and sisters are quite a tasty food. Cannibalism is not uncommon among young spiders.

At each stage of growth, spiders shed or molt their skin. Once they reach adulthood, they no longer molt.

Fascinating Facts

- Spider silk is the strongest of all natural fibers. It compares favorably with steel and is twice as strong as Kevlar of the same weight.

- Baby spiders (spiderlings) often disperse by jumping from an elevated position, emitting strands of silk and letting the wind carry them away. Some adult spiders will also disperse by catching a ride on the wind. This method of moving is referred to as ballooning. Ballooning is most commonly observed in autumn.

Thanks to Spiders

- When spiders are found in good numbers, sometimes thousands or millions per acre, they can help control insects that cause damage to agricultural crops.

- Some cultures, such as the Piaroa Indians in South America, actually eat large spiders and consider them a delicacy.

- Spider venom has been used in designing new drugs for health care.

Myth Busters

MYTH: A spider bit me last night while I was asleep. It couldn't have been anything else.

This is a widespread superstition. It is highly unusual for a spider to come into your bed. (Unless you sleep on the basement or garage floor!) In the unlikely event that a spider gets into your bed, it will not seek to bite you. If you happen to roll onto one, it might bite, but it's not likely.

According to some emergency room personnel, unexplained swelling or skin irritation is often blamed on a "spider bite." Nevertheless, when patients are asked if they actually saw a spider, they almost always say no. Research has shown that over 80 percent of suspected spider bites are caused by other insects, ticks, or by medical conditions.

Why They Bite

The primary reason a spider bites is to kill its prey, and almost all species of spiders are venomous. The venom helps them quickly kill or paralyze their prey. When a spider bites a human, it is not interested in wrapping you in silk; it is strictly a defensive act. Spiders are generally very timid around humans and will skitter away quickly if disturbed.

THINK TWICE

Think twice before calling a daddy longlegs a spider. They are nonvenomous arachnids that belong to a group called harvestmen.

Think twice about stepping on a spider caught indoors. By carefully catching and releasing the spider outside, you will model caring behavior to your children and others.

Around the world there is a universal belief that it is unlucky to kill a spider. In fact, there is an old English rhyme that speaks to such compassion toward spiders: "If you wish to live and thrive, let a spider run alive."

How They Bite

Actually, spiders don't bite, they inject. The spider's mouth is located directly below its eyes. Their large jaws are called chelicerae, and these vertical structures are often lined with small teeth and tipped with 2 fangs. In most spiders, these jaws swing inward from the sides to grasp prey. In some larger spider species, the jaws swing downward to pin down prey.

A spider's venom is secreted through the fangs into the prey, but spiders less than $5/16$ of an inch can't bite you, as they are too small. Pretty much all spiders larger than $5/16$ of an inch can bite humans, but most usually *won't*. Those that can break your skin will sometimes inject harmless venom, and some will not inject venom at all. Most spider bites are less painful than a bee sting, but some people are more sensitive to bites than others.

How Afraid Should I Be?

In the Rocky Mountain region, only the widow spiders are capable of delivering nasty bites. A very shy group of species, the widow spiders are typically not aggressive, but they will bite when accidentally trapped, disturbed or threatened. Usually, they prefer to retreat.

black widow

Widow spiders are often found hanging upside down in their tangled webs. The female delivers the more serious, but rarely lethal, bite. She has a round, shiny black abdomen with a red hourglass-shaped marking on the underside of her belly. Her bite might feel like a pinprick. The bite site might swell slightly and bear faint red marks. Within a few hours the pain intensifies and stiffness begins. Other symptoms of the neurotoxic venom include chills, fever, nausea and severe abdominal pain.

The hobo spider is another species to be aware of in the Rocky Mountains region. This widespread spider has its origins in Europe and gets its name from its habit of hitching rides from place to place. It has a larger body than the black widow, long legs and 2 appendages that resemble boxing gloves (these are actually sex organs).

hobo

The hobo spider constructs a web that looks like a funnel. Like widow spiders, the hobo prefers to flee when disturbed. The hobo spider is slightly venomous, but it is not a spider to be feared. When biting, it often injects no venom; this is called a dry bite. If venom is injected, the bite will turn red and swell.

brown recluse

The brown recluse spider delivers the most dangerous bite in the United States. It is *not* native to the Rocky Mountain region. However, there have been rare incidents where brown recluse spiders have accidentally been transported miles from their normal range on cargo. Colored tan to dark brown, it is approximately 1/2 inch long. It bears a distinctive, dark violin-shaped marking on top of the front body section (cephalothorax) and has 3 pairs of eyes. Almost all other species of spiders in this region have 4 pairs of eyes.

Several hours after a somewhat painless bite, a blister forms and the surrounding skin begins to darken and swell. The venom of the brown recluse can cause extensive tissue damage. It normally takes up to 2 months for such a bite to heal.

Preventing Spider Bites

- Avoid handling spiders with your bare hands. When removing spiders from your home, gently cover them with a glass or jar, slide a piece of paper underneath and release them outdoors.
- Don't reach into dusty, dark recesses with your bare hands.

Treatment of Bites

- If possible, capture the biting spider so it can be properly identified. In the highly unlikely event that a widow spider bites you, capture it for positive identification and seek immediate medical attention.
- Clean and wash the bite site with soap and hot water. Apply ice and elevate the affected area.
- To guard against infection, apply an antiseptic lotion or cream.
- Most bites improve within a few hours to 3 days.
- Seek medical attention if symptoms persist or worsen. This is especially important with children.

BOTTOM LINE

Spiders are timid around people and skitter away if disturbed. If one does bite you, it is strictly in self-defense. In the Rocky Mountain region, most spider bites are harmless, but if a widow spider or a brown recluse spider bites you, seek medical attention immediately.

Deer and Horse Flies

Every summer, I shudder when I hear the simple declaration, "The deer flies are out." Along with horse flies, these persistent biters can turn an otherwise perfect day at the beach, in the garden, or in the boat into a sore test of endurance.

Sometimes, though, they help us see the larger drama of life. I recall one day in my garden as I crawled down a row of peas, deer flies flew laps around my head and occasionally stole in for a quick bite. Suddenly I heard a clattering of wings just above my head. I tipped my head to sneak a peek. A dragonfly! Soon a second joined it. I heard more clattering and even felt slight taps on my hat. They were picking off deer flies that were alighting on my head! In a sense, I had become a dragonfly feeder. By attracting the deer flies, I provided easy pickings for the predators. What had been a pest to me was sustenance for the dragonflies.

About Deer and Horse Flies

This is a well-represented group of flies. There are approximately 4,300 species in the world, with more than 160 species of horse flies and over 110 types of deer flies occurring in the continental United States. Both deer and horse flies have similar life cycles.

deer fly   horse fly

Deer flies, sometimes called yellow flies, are smaller than horse flies. They measure about $1/4$–$3/8$ inch long. They are commonly tan colored with distinct dark patches on their wings. Their antennae are slightly longer than the heads. They are strong fliers and are usually not solitary.

The larger horse fly averages $1/2$–$1^1/4$ inches long and is more robust. Its wings have no patches and are uniformly cloudy. The antennae are shorter than the head and thick at the base. Horse fly eyes are large and appear colorful.

Both flies are dependent on wetlands, such as marshes, ponds or slow-moving streams, to complete their life cycles. As adults, they can cover wide areas. Deer flies are particularly fond of brush, woods and meadows. Horse flies tend to be more common around larger bodies of water such as lakes.

Life and Times . . .

In the Rocky Mountain region, deer flies typically make their appearance in late spring to early summer. Prior to mating, males and females feed on plant

deer fly laying eggs

nectars and juices. After mating, the female seeks a meal of blood.

Males are rarely seen but can be distinguished from females by their large compound eyes, which touch each other; the female's eyes are distinctly separate.

The female lays a single mass of 100–800 eggs on the underside of a leaf or on the stem of a plant growing out of a wetland. Freshly laid egg masses are whitish and soon darken upon exposure to air.

In 2–3 days, the eggs hatch and the larvae drop down into the water or mud to complete their development. The last larval stage spends the winter dormant in the wetland. The following spring, the larvae shed their skin and proceed to the pupal stage. It takes 1–3 weeks for the adult fly to pupate. Most deer and horse flies pupate on the edge of marshes, swamps and ponds.

The larvae of deer flies feed on insects and plant material. On the other hand, all studied species of horse fly larvae eat other insects.

Fascinating Facts

- Only female deer and horse flies bite.

- The mating flight for these flies is generally in the early morning. The female requires a blood meal only after mating.

- Some of the larger species of horse flies require 2–3 years to develop in an aquatic environment before emerging as adults.

Thanks to Deer and Horse Flies

- Both of these flies are important prey species for many birds and other insects.

- The aquatic larvae of deer and horse flies provide a food source for many species of fish.

- The males of each species are important plant pollinators.

Myth Busters

MYTH: Swatting at deer flies will chase them away.

It won't. In fact, the motion will agitate them and probably attract more.

Why They Bite

With some exceptions, the female deer or horse fly needs to feed on blood in order to produce viable eggs. Like all other biting flies, they only bite during daylight hours—lying in ambush in the shade of brush or trees and swarming around any passing potential host. They zero in on a target by noting movement, the release of carbon dioxide (emitted when you exhale) and odors such as fragrant perfumes or shampoos.

How They Bite

Deer and horse fly bites are painfully similar. A tiny pair of blade-like mandibles lacerate the skin, causing blood to flow—which is lapped up with

horse fly

a spongelike mouthpart. Like mosquitoes, these flies incorporate an anticoagulant into the bite to make the wound bleed more freely. A bite often results in a small red welt that might persist for several days. Slight swelling and itchiness may occur at the site of the bite.

If deer or horse flies are numerous enough, they will change your outdoor plans. Of the 2 species of flies, I consider the deer fly a greater pest. Some folks claim, "A deer fly is a black fly on steroids!"

How Afraid Should I Be?

Deer and horse fly bites are generally not serious injuries. But they can result in open wounds and a possible secondary infection. Aggressively scratching the affected area can make matters worse.

THINK TWICE

Think twice about strolling into the brush or hiking near a wetland during fly season. Whatever you do, don't forget your hat!

And think twice about being the first person in line when on a hike . . . you will receive more of the flies' wrath than those following.

Even if deer flies only occasionally bite you, they are extremely annoying as they swirl in a horde around your head. Ironically, they seem to flock to moving targets. In other words, if you restrict your movements you will be less of a target. Luckily, neither the horse nor deer fly will enter your tent or home to seek you out. If you have ever noticed a wayward deer or horse fly in a house or vehicle, they are usually bouncing off a window trying to get out.

Preventing Deer and Horse Fly Bites

- The best prevention for keeping both of these biting flies at bay is to cover up. When deer fly season is underway, I don't leave home without a hat.

- Repellents do not work.

- Avoid deer and horse fly habitat during midsummer.

- Some outdoor workers and enthusiasts have good success with adhesive deer fly patches. Nontoxic and odorless, the double-sided patches work like portable fly strips. Press one to the back of your hat or cap and it will attract circling deer flies—which find themselves stuck upon landing.

- Deer flies typically go after the tallest person in a group, as well as the one walking in front. Use this tip wisely. If the hike leader turns to you complaining about the deer flies, swing your hands wildly at imaginary antagonists and grumble loudly!

- I have had some success sticking the stems of tall bracken ferns down the back of my shirt, so the front projects like an umbrella above my head. This creates a canopy of ferns over my head that does a decent job of distracting the deer flies. I think it looks cool, too.

- I have a neighbor who swears that affixing a blue—yes, blue—Dixie cup to the top of her head attracts deer flies to the cup instead of her head. (I'll stick to ferns, myself.)

Treatment of Bites

Wash bites with warm water and soap. Benadryl and other anti-itch or anti-inflammatory compounds, lotions and creams can provide itching relief.

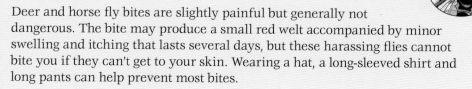

BOTTOM LINE

Deer and horse fly bites are slightly painful but generally not dangerous. The bite may produce a small red welt accompanied by minor swelling and itching that lasts several days, but these harassing flies cannot bite you if they can't get to your skin. Wearing a hat, a long-sleeved shirt and long pants can help prevent most bites.

Hornets, Wasps and Yellow Jackets

No group of insects urges humans to retreat faster than wasps, hornets and yellow jackets. They wear their stripes well. We have come to learn that the distinct pattern of belted stripes encircling the bodies of this fierce crew is a clear visual warning to "Watch out!" While most encounters are benign, their stings are painful and, for some people, allergic reactions to the venom can be life-threatening.

About Hornets, Wasps and Yellow Jackets

Like honeybees and bumblebees, these groups of thin-waisted and mostly hairless insects live in social colonies made up of workers (infertile females), queens and males.

bald-faced hornet

paper wasp

yellow jacket

Life and Times . . .

Colonies of hornets, wasps and yellow jackets remain active for only 1 summer, after which the fertilized queens fly away to start more colonies. Other colony members die at the end of the summer, and the nest is not reused.

Fertilized queens winter in protected places such as hollow logs, stumps, under bark, in leaf litter, in abandoned animal dens and in man-made structures. They emerge in the warm days of late April and early May to select a nest site and build a small paper nest in which to lay their eggs.

After her first brood hatches, a queen feeds the young larvae for about 18–20 days. These young will eventually pupate and emerge around mid-June as the colony's first group of workers. Infertile females, their jobs will include foraging for food, defending the nest and caring for the queen's subsequent hatches of larvae. Each cell in the nest may be used for 2 or 3 batches of broods.

The larvae's primary diet consists of protein-rich foods such as insects, meats and fish. Adults are particularly fond of fruits, flower nectar and tree sap, which provide ample doses of sugars and carbohydrates.

The queen stays with her nest throughout the summer, laying eggs. Eventually she might build an empire of several thousand workers. In late August and early September, she creates cells where future queens and males are produced. They are cared for and fed by the sterile workers before leaving the colony in the fall for a mating flight. After mating, the males die and fertilized queens look for protected sites to spend the winter. The old queen from the summer nest dies, and the workers begin to behave erratically until social order breaks down. With the onset of winter, the remaining colony dies.

BALD-FACED HORNET IDENTIFICATION

The bald-faced hornet is similar to a paper wasp and the yellow jacket. Two primary differences involve the hornet's nest and physical appearance.

- The bald-faced hornet's nest is ball- or oval-shaped and can be larger than a basketball. Nests are most often constructed on a tree limb or shrub branch. Hidden by summer foliage, they are most easily viewed after the leaves fall in autumn.

- The hornet itself is large, black and thin waisted. It is named for its distinctive white or "bald" face.

bald-faced hornet nest

paper wasp nest

PAPER WASP IDENTIFICATION

The queen paper wasp creates a single layer of cells that is attached by a stem to the underside of eaves, benches and other protected overhangs.

Paper wasps, like yellow jackets, are striped in yellow and black. However, they are slightly larger (particularly in the abdomen) than yellow jackets.

YELLOW JACKET IDENTIFICATION

Of the 3 groups mentioned here, yellow jackets are the only ones that often nest underground. Sometimes they nest behind the siding of a building or in a building crevice.

yellow jacket underground nest

Fascinating Facts

- Wasps and hornets make their papery nests by chewing on tiny pieces of wood, bark or even cardboard. They add their saliva to the chewed wood and "paint" it into a smooth, thin material used for making the nest. The various colors of the rather artful nest are determined by the source of the wood.

- Of the approximately 15,000 species of stinging wasps in the world, 95 percent of them do not sting humans.

- After the nests freeze in the fall, any remaining larvae are dead. These frozen treats are high in fat and are desirable food items for squirrels, skunks and even birds such as woodpeckers and blue jays.

- The stinger on this group of insects has evolved from the long, sharp portion of the insect called the ovipositor. It is also the mechanism from which eggs are deposited.

Thanks to Hornets, Wasps and Yellow Jackets

- Worker wasps and hornets feed on caterpillars and other insects that are often harmful to human food crops. These include corn earworms, army worms, tobacco hornworms, house flies, blowflies and harmful caterpillars.

- Although they lack the pollen-carrying structures of bees, yellow jackets can be minor pollinators when visiting flowers.

- They often eat the flesh of dead animals, making them important members of the cleanup crew.

Myth Busters

MYTH: All bees and wasps sting.

Many wasps are non-stinging and most do not sting humans. Only female wasps are capable of inflicting a sting. Males are rarely seen since their function is to mate during the fall mating flight. And just because a wasp or a hornet looks scary doesn't mean it will sting you. The ichneumon wasp has a long ovipositor (a tube for depositing eggs) at the end of its body, which looks a lot like a stinger, but it's not. The wasp drills the ovipositor into soft or rotting wood and lays its eggs.

Myth: Just because an insect looks like a wasp or hornet, it is one.

Actually, many harmless insects look a lot like wasps or hornets. Many insect species mimic the colors of their feistier neighbors in order to protect themselves. If an insect looks like a yellow jacket, wasp or hornet, birds and other predators think twice before attacking, as the predators see the bright colors and sometimes shy away. But many innocent insects are often confused for wasps or hornets and unfairly swatted. Just because an insect looks like a wasp or a hornet, it doesn't mean it is one.

Why They Sting

These groups of insects sting primarily to kill prey. They are predators. Secondly, they use the sting to defend themselves or the colony. They simply do not seek out humans to randomly sting. With that said, while your intentions might be totally innocent, if a hornet, wasp or yellow jacket perceives you as a threat, it will sting you.

bald-faced hornet

How They Sting

The stinger is located in the tip of the abdomen. Unlike honeybees—which can only sting once—hornets, wasps and yellow jackets do not lose their stinger and can sting repeatedly. The dose of toxin delivered is less than that of a honeybee and is reduced with each sting. When a hornet, wasp or yellow jacket stings, the 2 halves of the abdomen casing open up to allow the stinger to emerge. The stinger is made up of a piercing stylet and 2 tiny flanking lancets.

The sting happens when the stinger is thrust into the victim and the micro-lancets move back and forth like a saw. These lancets are slightly barbed at the edges. Anchored in the flesh, the moving lancets trigger a pumping action at the end of the abdomen, causing the venom sac to pump venom into the wound. Since hornets, wasps and yellow jackets have smaller barbs on their lancets than honeybees, they can pull the shaft out and fly happily away. On the other hand, the honeybee's stinger stays fixed in the flesh. When it pulls away, it literally pulls out the stinger and venom sac. The injury results in the bee's death.

The sting of hornets contains acetylcholine, which stimulates pain nerves more than the stings of other wasps and bees—so hornet stings can be a bit more painful.

> **THINK TWICE**
>
> Think twice about aggressively shooing away hornets, wasps or yellow jackets from your picnic. Flailing your arms and swinging at the insect might provoke defensive behavior and that could result in a sting.
>
> Think twice about trying to kill a hornet, wasp or yellow jacket that you discover while driving your car. Slowly pull over to the side of the road and open the windows and doors so it can fly out. You are in far more danger of initiating a car accident if you try to get the insect out while you're behind the wheel.

How Afraid Should I Be?

There is no need to fear these insects. Respect, yes, but not fear. Most of their lives are spent trying to make a living, searching for food for themselves and the brood. Any attack on you is time spent away from foraging.

Minimize attacks through avoidance, staying calm and being alert. For example, in late summer foraging yellow jackets become a nuisance when they change from eating meat to a diet of ripe, rotting fruits, human garbage, sweet drinks and picnic foods. By understanding their behavior and responding accordingly, we can prevent most attacks.

Preventing Stings

- Hornets, wasps and particularly yellow jackets are very defensive around their nests. If you locate nests, simply note them and avoid them, telling other people who frequent the area. I would not recommend nest eradication unless the nest poses a threat to humans. I have had very good success in preventing wasp nest construction by applying a thin film of petroleum jelly underneath picnic tabletops and seats, deck benches, etc. If you must get rid of a nest, plan to remove it early in the morning or later in the evening, when cooler temperatures have ushered the inhabitants into the nest. If you are using a chemical, read and carefully follow the label directions.

wasp

- Avoid fragrant soaps, shampoos, perfumes, aftershaves and colognes. Hornets, wasps and yellow jackets are sometimes attracted to them.

- Keep children from throwing rocks at nests or spraying them with water. Avoid making loud noises or disturbing the nests.

- Some folks have luck with yellow jacket/hornet traps that are placed outside a home or near a picnic site. The sweet bait lures them into the trap, from which there is no exit.

Treatment of Stings

- Wash the site of the sting with soap and water, and apply ice to minimize swelling and pain. Mixing a solution of $1/2$ teaspoon meat tenderizer with 1 teaspoon water and placing it on the wound can minimize discomfort.

- Pay close attention to how you feel after a sting. Allergic reactions to the venom occur in approximately 1 percent of the human population. If someone else is stung, watch them for about an hour. Seek immediate medical attention if you notice any change in breathing, scratchiness in the throat or symptoms of hives. In the meantime, keep the victim quiet, calm and as still as possible.

- If you know that you or one of your family members are allergic to bee or wasp venom, ask your doctor for a prescription for either an Anaphylaxis Emergency Treatment Kit or an EpiPen. Both contain injectable adrenaline (epinephrine) for allergic reactions. Carry your kit or EpiPen with you at all times during the peak hornet, wasp and yellow jacket season. Carefully follow instructions to administer the epinephrine.

BOTTOM LINE

Hornets, wasps and yellow jackets deserve respect, not fear. Most of their lives are spent trying to find food for themselves and their broods. St⁻ are purely defensive attacks that can be minimized through avoidanc⁻ calm and being alert.

Honeybees

The honeybee is arguably the most valuable insect to our well-being. Not only do honeybees provide us with a wonderful sweetener, but they also add approximately $15 billion in value to agricultural crops such as apples, almonds, berries, other fruits and vegetables.

On the other hand, the honeybee is likely responsible for more human deaths or close calls in the Rocky Mountain region than any other wild animal. Every year approximately 50 people die in the United States from allergic reactions to bee and wasp stings.

About Honeybees

Seven species of honeybees produce and store honey and build colonial nests out of wax produced by the colony workers. The western honeybee is the subspecies that has been domesticated for honey and wax production. Not native to North America, honeybees were introduced from Europe nearly 400 years ago by early colonists.

Life and Times . . .

Generally, most of the bees in a colony or hive all have the same mother; she is known as the queen bee. There is 1 queen per colony. She makes 1–2 mating flights in her life. After mating with 1 or more males (drones) she is able to store millions of sperm cells in her body. She is capable of living for several years and during that period she will lay tens of thousands of eggs.

Most of the bees in the colony are non-fertile females. These worker bees live only for 6 weeks in the summer or for 4–9 months during the winter months. They are highly organized and assume specific roles: some bees forage for nectar and pollen, while others guard the colony, or serve as construction workers, helping build the hive. Still other workers serve as nurse bees; a few even tend to the queen as her royal attendants. While we might think it is grim, the chore of cleaning dead bees out of the hive is simply a natural task for another group of bees.

The bumblebee has a similar life cycle. Like honeybees, they also produce honey and live in colonies. If you see a large bumblebee buzzing loudly among spring's first flowers, it is likely a queen bee gathering pollen for her underground nest.

Of the entire hive, only the fertilized queen survives the winter. She lays her eggs on pollen and covers them

honeybee hive

with wax. After 4–5 days, the eggs hatch and the larvae feed on the stored pollen. The larvae pupate into cocoons, and after nearly 2 weeks, the queen strips off the wax and the bees emerge. These are infertile workers.

Later in the summer the queen lays eggs that produce males and fertile females. They will leave the nest and mate. Only queens that have successfully mated will overwinter. All others, including the summer queen, will die.

Fascinating Facts

- Even when separated from the bee, the venom sac continues to pump venom into the skin for approximately 2 minutes.

- Only female honeybees are equipped with stingers; stingers are slightly barbed.

- A bumblebee's loud buzzing is not caused by the movement of its wings, but is due to the vibration of the bee's flight muscles. Bumblebees and honeybees can make their characteristic buzzing sound even when the wings are detached from the muscles.

- Like other insects, a bumblebee's body temperature is determined by the local air temperature, and it must warm up before flying.

- Bees have 2 stomachs. One is dedicated to storing flower nectar and the other is their regular stomach. When full, the nectar-bearing stomach weighs almost as much as the bee. Bees must visit 100–1,500 flowers in order to "fill up" on nectar.

Thanks to Honeybees

- Some plants need honeybee pollination as much as they need water and sunlight. The U.S. Department of Agriculture estimates that one-third of our daily diet relies on insect pollination, and honeybees perform 80 percent of that pollination.

- Bee venom contains a very potent anti-inflammatory agent and is used by many people to manage joint pain, arthritis and even multiple sclerosis.

- Bees pollinate many types of plants that cause allergy problems for some folks. Some people claim that honey produced from the nectar of these plants' flowers helps minimize the misery.

- Beekeeping is a vital occupation for thousands of people. Bees help produce a variety of products, including honey, pollen and beeswax.

Myth Busters

MYTH: A honeybee can sting you over and over.

When a bee pulls away after stinging you, she pulls away a portion of her abdomen, resulting in her death. She is willing to give up her life to defend herself or the hive.

> **THINK TWICE**
>
> Think twice before you investigate a beehive without supervision from a beekeeper and without the protection of proper beekeeping clothing.
>
> Think twice before picking a lovely bouquet of flowers. Carefully inspect the blossoms to make sure you don't disturb a foraging bee.

Why They Sting

Bees sting for two primary reasons: to defend themselves and to defend their colony. Like wasps, hornets and yellow jackets, bees do not go out looking for victims to sting.

How They Sting

A bee's stinger is a formidable weapon. It consists of 2 sharp, curved blades with 8–10 barbs near the tip. A narrow duct is formed when the blades are positioned next to each other. This duct serves as the channel from which the venom is delivered from the venom sac. Muscles near the stinger force the barb into the flesh and then muscles pump venom into the flesh.

When you are stung, the stinger emits a pheromonal alarm (a mixture of chemical compounds designed to provoke a certain behavior) that is detected by other bees; this quickly warns other bees to maintain alertness and prepare to attack.

How Afraid Should I Be?

Given that honeybees and bumblebees are not normally aggressive and are far more interested in working for the welfare of their hive, they are not usually a problem. However, if you know or suspect you are allergic to bee venom, be proactive and seek a doctor who will prescribe the proper medication. Then it is up to you to have it accessible when outdoors. Most human deaths occur in the first hour after the sting occurs.

Preventing Bee Stings

- If a bee is flying around you, simply ignore it or gently urge it away.

- Flailing your arms and swinging at the bee might provoke a defensive behavior, and that could result in a sting.

- Avoid strongly scented skin products, soaps and shampoos.

- If you are working in a flower garden or find yourself anywhere that bees gather, perhaps the best preparation is to simply wear proper clothing that minimizes skin exposure. Mosquito repellents are ineffective against bees.

honeybee covered with pollen

- Bees sometimes swarm in the most unusual places. Officials at a major league baseball game once had to call a timeout while a beekeeper removed a swarm that had clustered in one of the dugouts!

- Swarms of bees are rarely aggressive, and you should be patient and let them move on their way. Sometimes the swarm can linger for a couple of days. Please *do not* kill them with a pesticide. At the very least, contact a local beekeeper; they will be happy to remove the bees to create a new hive for their beekeeping yard.

Treatment of Stings

- Immediately remove the stinger and venom sac by carefully scraping the stinger with a fingernail or knife blade. *Do not* grasp the stinger with your fingers or a tweezers or you will only force venom into the wound.

- You can also purchase an extractor to remove the venom from the site of the sting. However, most stings do not happen with a first aid kit nearby, and this is the likely place to find a venom extractor.

- Wash the site of the sting with soap and water and apply ice to minimize swelling and pain. Mixing a solution $1/2$ teaspoon meat tenderizer and 1 teaspoon water and placing it on the wound can minimize discomfort.

- Pay close attention to how you feel after a sting. Allergic reactions to the bee's venom occur in approximately 1 percent of the human population. If someone else is stung, watch them closely and seek immediate medical attention if you notice any change in breathing, if they complain of scratchiness in the throat or exhibit symptoms of hives. In the meantime, keep the victim quiet, calm and as still as possible.

- If you or one of your family members is allergic to bee stings, ask your doctor for a prescription for either an Anaphylaxis Emergency Treatment Kit or an EpiPen. Both contain injectable adrenaline (epinephrine) for allergic reactions. Carry your kit or EpiPen with you at all times during the peak bee season. Carefully follow instructions to administer the epinephrine.

BOTTOM LINE

There is no reason to fear honeybees and bumblebees. They only sting to defend themselves or their colony. When a bee buzzes around you, enjoy the unique "music" of this beneficial little insect, or gently urge it away. Flailing your arms might provoke defensive behavior—and a sting.

Giant Water Bugs

There are approximately 100 species of giant water bugs in the world. Though fierce-looking, they are often prepared as a human food item in parts of Asia and elsewhere. At the Typhoon Restaurant in Santa Monica, California, you can get a pair of chicken-stuffed water bugs, deep-fried and seasoned Thai style, for $8!

About Giant Water Bugs

Its name sounds like something out of a science fiction movie, and indeed the giant water bug is an oversize, nasty-looking insect. Also known as a Toe Biter or Fish Killer, it can grow to about 4 inches in length.

Humans most often see giant water bugs on land, but they spend most of their lives in the water—where your chances of a bite are greatest. While a bite from this insect can be painful, it is highly unlikely to happen. This sinister-looking bug avoids human contact whenever possible.

Life and Times . . .

Giant water bugs (*Lethocerus sp.*) are the Goliaths of the Rocky Mountain insects. As their name suggests, they live in water, preferring still or slow-flowing areas with an abundance of vegetation. Voracious predators, they hunt by ambush from their hideouts in aquatic plants or dead leaves on the bottom of the wetland.

They grasp other insects, tadpoles, small fish or salamanders with their large strong front legs, then inject venom produced from their salivary glands. These toxins paralyze the prey and liquefy its insides—which are then sucked up through the giant water bug's straw-like beak.

In some species of giant water bugs, the males carry hundreds of eggs on their backs. The females fasten the eggs there with a glue-like substance. The male fans water over them with his legs; this behavior, called brooding, reduces the risk of having the eggs dry up, keeps water flowing over the eggs and protects them from potential predators.

Despite their size, giant water bugs are hard to spot unless you're looking for them. Although you may catch a glimpse of one recharging its air supply at the surface, they spend much of their time on the bottom or hiding among the leaves and stalks of aquatic plants.

Fascinating Facts

- Giant water bugs often take wing at night in search of a new home or mate. But such flights are risky: entomologists believe artificial lights confuse the insects, causing them to fly around the lights until they die.

- Adults breathe air at the surface using 2 short tubes located at the tip of the abdomen. The air is stored in a bubble under the wings, where it supplies oxygen during dives.

- Giant water bugs belong to a rather notorious family tree. They are related to assassin bugs, boxelder bugs and stink bugs.

Thanks to Giant Water Bugs

- These large insects provide food for other predators such as herons, egrets, raccoons, mink and a variety of fish species.

- Giant water bugs also help keep populations of invertebrates in check.

Myth Busters

MYTH: They look scary, so they must be mean.

Yes, giant water bugs look nasty. And they will bite when captured, cornered or otherwise harassed. But they don't go looking for trouble; in fact, they prefer to retreat, hide or even play dead when threatened.

Why They Bite

Unlike mosquitoes and deer flies, giant water bugs don't hunt humans. So unless you resemble a minnow or tadpole, you'll most likely be bitten because you're a threat.

How They Bite

The giant water bug pierces its prey (as well as wayward toes or fingers) with its sharp mouthpart. Toxin is injected into the flesh by a needlelike beak. It may also pinch with its powerful front legs.

How Afraid Should I Be?

Unless you actively seek out and handle giant water bugs, it's unlikely you'll be bitten, and if you avoid areas with aquatic vegetation, a bite is even less likely. And if you stay out of the water, there's almost no chance of being bitten.

If you are bitten, grit your teeth. The injected toxin causes what is reportedly the most painful of all insect bites. It is often accompanied by inflammation below the bite. Most people quickly recover and suffer no lasting ill effects. However, because there is venom in the bite, there is the possibility of an anaphylactic reaction.

Preventing Giant Water Bug Bites

Since this beefy bug hides out in weeds in still or slow-moving water, the best way to avoid it is to stay out of the water, particularly weedy areas.

THINK TWICE

Think twice if you're tempted to pick up a giant water bug for a closer look—you're risking a painful bite. If you simply must inspect one, keep your fingers away from its head and mouthparts. And never assume a "dead" bug is safe to handle. It may only be feigning death.

- If you feel compelled to pick one up to inspect it, do so carefully! Firmly hold the insect between your thumb and forefinger, grasping its sides or back and underside—never the head.

- Wearing water shoes or an old pair of tennis shoes while wading will help protect your toes and feet from encounters with giant water bugs.

Treatment of Bites

- If you, or anyone you know, has an allergic reaction to stings and bites, you should get a prescription for an EpiPen. The EpiPen is a combined syringe and needle that injects a single dose of medication. Be sure your doctor shows you and other members of your family how to use the EpiPen.

- Watch the giant water bug bite site for several days. If the wound becomes discolored and the flesh appears to rot, seek medical assistance.

BOTTOM LINE

Giant water bugs look scary but unless you resemble a tadpole, they're not out to get you. If you don't handle or otherwise harass them, it's unlikely that you'll be bitten. The risk factor drops even more if you avoid areas with aquatic plants, and falls off the chart on dry land.

Leeches

"If there is anything in the world I hate, it's leeches. Oh, the filthy little devils!"

—Humphrey Bogart as Charlie in the movie, *The African Queen*

I am haunted by the image of Bogart standing on the deck of the *African Queen* covered in leeches. And yet for over 2,000 years, leeches have played a profound role in treating various human ailments. How is it that these same graceful swimming animals don't inspire applause for their role in medicine?

About Leeches

In the Rocky Mountain region, adult leeches are large, dark, segmented aquatic worms with a strong sucker at each end. (Young leeches are small.) The front sucker, where the mouth is located, can be very small. Many leeches are strong swimmers as evidenced by their rippling movements through the water.

They are commonly found hiding in muck or submerged vegetation in quiet sections of lakes, ponds, marshes and other wetlands.

Life and Times . . .

Leeches are parasites and must feed on blood from a host to survive. Some feed on the blood of humans and other mammals, while others feed on fish, turtles, frogs or birds. Some leeches even feed on other blood-engorged leeches.

Leeches are unique in that there are no females and no males! They are hermaphrodites. That means they have both male and female sex organs. When they mate, they intertwine their bodies and deposit sperm in the other's clitellum. (This is the raised band where the sex organs are located. It is very obvious in an earthworm.)

After fertilization takes place, the clitellum secretes a tough, jellylike cocoon that contains nutrients. The eggs are deposited in this mass. The released cocoon is either buried or attached to a stick or rock. After weeks or even months, the young leeches emerge looking like tiny adults. Leeches usually die after 1 or 2 reproductive episodes.

Fascinating Facts

- In 2003, a boy in Boston had his ear bitten off by a dog. After the ear was reattached there were problems with blood pooling around the wound site. After exhausting other treatments, doctors applied leeches around the wound. It worked, and now most large hospitals, including the world-famous Mayo Clinic, use leeches in some medical procedures.

- In the nineteenth century, leeches were used to forecast bad weather. Leeches breathe through their body wall and they position themselves to take in dissolved oxygen. Leeches kept in a jar will swim close to the surface when there is a fall in atmospheric pressure, which often foretells the arrival of rainy, stormy weather.

- In the nineteenth century, barbers not only cut hair, they often relieved patients of supposedly "bad" blood. They did so with the help of leeches. The familiar red-and-white striped pole found outside a barbershop represented blood and bandages.

Thanks to Leeches

- Many fish, wading birds (such as herons and egrets) and other animals feed on leeches and bloodsuckers.

- The bite of a leech produces a small, bleeding wound that mimics blood flow. Consequently, the leech is becoming more and more valuable for surgery.

Myth Busters

MYTH: Water-resistant insect repellents will keep leeches off you.

There is no evidence of any repellent or home remedy that will effectively discourage leeches from feeding on you. These include coating exposed body parts with bath soap, eucalyptus oil or lemon juice.

Why They Bite

The soft, stealthy bite of a leech is simply to gain access to blood. They do not defend themselves by biting.

How They Bite

After detecting potential prey with the help of sensory organs on the surface of its head and body, the leech "inchworms" slowly toward its quarry and then gently attaches itself. The leech's "mouth" is made up of 3 jaws. Arranged in a Y-shaped pattern, they work together in a sawing motion. It's a wickedly effective combination, since each jaw can contain about 100 teeth! The leech's saliva is like a pharmacy, containing an assortment of chemicals that help it feed. There's an anesthetic to minimize the pain. (If a leech can be sneaky about biting, you won't discover it—and a leech needs time to "download" its blood meal.) There is also a blood thinner (anticoagulant) to maximize blood flow, and a vasodilator that encourages the opening of blood vessels for easier bleeding. To further speed the process, a spreading factor moves these chemicals easily and quickly. Finally, a bacterium in the leech's gut helps it digest the blood—what a marvelous organism.

How Afraid Should I Be?

You need not be very afraid of a leech attaching itself to you. Firstly, it is a rare occurrence and the bite has no venom and is a very superficial wound. There is no evidence that leeches transmit any diseases.

Preventing Leech Bites

- Stay out of mucky wetlands. If you wade into likely leech habitat, wear appropriate clothing to make it impossible for a leech to find your skin.

Treatment of Bites

- If the leech is still attached, the best way to remove it is to press your finger on the skin next to the leech's sucker (mouthparts); next, gently but firmly push your finger toward its sucker and use your fingernail to dislodge it.

- Wash the bite with soap and water. Apply a bandage if necessary. Anticoagulants from the leech might cause oozing of blood for several hours.

- Some irritation and itching might occur after the bite. Benadryl and other anti-itching compounds can provide some relief. Watch for possible infection or allergic reaction. Seek medical attention if a change in the wound occurs.

THINK TWICE

Avoid old-school methods of leech removal such as applying salt or stoically yanking the critter loose. Sprinkling salt on a leech attached to your skin might cause more discomfort than the actual bite. Worse, aggressively pulling on a leech could cause it to literally squeeze its stomach contents into the open wound. Gross!

BOTTOM LINE

Don't let a fear of leeches keep you out of the water. There's no reason to be afraid. "Attachments" are rare, unless you regularly wade barefoot in mucky, "leechy" habitat. Their bite has no venom and is harmless.

Scorpions

Scorpions have played a major role in the mythology of many different cultures. Serqet, the ancient Egyptian goddess of scorpions and venomous creatures, is often depicted wearing a headpiece in the shape of a scorpion, its characteristic stinger raised over its back. Several Greek legends involve the scorpion as well. In one, the great hunter Orion boasts that he could single-handedly hunt and kill every beast on earth. Artemis, the protector of life and the goddess of the hunt, enlisted the help of the scorpion to prove Orion wrong. The scorpion killed Orion with its venomous sting. In death, Orion was placed in the heavens, as was the scorpion (Scorpius), but Orion was placed far from Scorpius, and Scorpius chases Orion across the heavens; as one constellation rises, the other sets.

About Scorpions

Like ticks, chiggers and spiders, scorpions are arachnids. A scorpion's slender, extended body is segmented and equipped with 8 jointed legs. Its tail is segmented as well and arches over the scorpion's back, and the tail is tipped with a venomous stinger. Scorpions in the Rocky Mountain region are less than 3 inches long.

Scorpions are efficient predators and prey upon small insects, spiders and even other scorpions. Despite their tough exoskeletons, scorpions are often prey themselves and are hunted by rodents, lizards, nocturnal birds (especially owls), bats and centipedes.

There are approximately 1,400 scorpion species in the world and 70 species in North America. There are fewer than 20 species in the Rocky Mountain region. Of these species, there is only 1 to be concerned about—the bark scorpion. Since it prefers arid habitats, it is found only rarely, in the southern part of the Rocky Mountain region. On rare occasions, scorpions are found outside of their natural range after they are accidentally transported in luggage or cargo.

Life and Times . . .

A scorpion's front claws, called pedipalps, are important appendages for securing prey and for dancing, an important courtship ritual. Contrary to popular belief, the pedipalps are not legs.

During courtship, male and female scorpions locate each other by pheromones and vibration. Once they locate each other and determine that they are of the opposite sex, the male grabs the female's pedipalps with his own and drags her around in what looks like a frantic dance. He does this until he finds a place where he can deposit his spermatophore (a capsule containing a mass of his spermatozoa). The female draws the spermatophore into the underside of her abdomen and the sperm is released.

bark scorpion

Once the mating is complete, the male and female will go their own ways. The male is usually quick to leave, likely to avoid being cannibalized by the female, although sexual cannibalism is infrequent with scorpions.

The fertilized female will not give birth for several months, and in some species gestation requires more than a year. Scorpions are unusual among arthropods in that all species are viviparous—the young are born alive and look like miniature adults.

THINK TWICE

Think twice about reaching under any debris or items that might harbor a resting scorpion.

When camping, think twice about putting on shoes or clothing that have been lying on the ground. Be sure to inspect them first or they might harbor an unexpected guest.

Unlike female ticks and spiders, which bear thousands of young, a female scorpion can bear anywhere from 1 to 100 young, though the average litter size is 8. The young stay with their mother until after they shed their skin for the first time (molt); this usually occurs after about 2 weeks. Scorpions must molt several times before reaching sexual maturity; most species molt 5–7 times.

Scorpions are unusually long-lived compared to other invertebrates. In the wild, scorpions live 2–6 years, with females generally living longer than males.

Fascinating Facts

- Scorpions have remained essentially unchanged since they first appeared in oceans over 400 million years ago. Those early marine scorpions had external lungs. One recently discovered scorpion fossil was $8^1/_2$ feet long!

- Scorpions use highly sensitive hairs and slits on their legs to measure ground vibrations to determine the size and position of their next meal.

- Scorpions naturally fluoresce under long-wave ultraviolet light, and can be found in the dark by using a flashlight with an ultraviolet bulb or LED (a blacklight). Scorpions can be seen from many feet away as a green-colored glow. Using a UV flashlight is by far the best way to find scorpions.

Thanks to Scorpions

- Scorpion venom has medical applications; some venom contains elements that alter the blood-clotting process, and research has shown that a synthetic version of a protein found in some scorpion venom can be used to treat brain cancer and tumors.

- In some countries, including Vietnam, scorpions are a specialty at restaurants and are used in making wine.

Myth Busters

MYTH: Scorpions will give you a painful pinch with their 2 claws.

While the front appendages might look like legs or nasty claws, they are called pedipalps. These pincerlike appendages are used to grasp prey, for defense and are used during mating. Bristles on the pedipalps also help detect air currents and vibrations.

MYTH: Scorpions are so aggressive they sometimes sting themselves to death.

A scorpion's formidable tail and stinger arch over its back, sometimes so much so that the scorpion seems in danger of stinging itself, but this doesn't happen.

Why They Sting

Scorpions use their venomous stinger for defending themselves or for killing their prey. They do not aggressively pursue and sting large mammals.

How They Sting

At first glance, a scorpion looks a little like a crab, and its claws look like they could deliver a painful pinch. Nevertheless, the stinger, not the claws, are the scorpion's primary weapon.

A scorpion uses its large pincers to grab its prey; then, it arches its tail over its body and whips its tail downward, driving the stinger into its prey. Sometimes it stings repeatedly, and it can regulate how much of its venom it injects with each sting. If it uses all of its venom, it takes several days to replenish its supply. A scorpion's venom consists of various concentrations of nerve, blood and kidney toxins. Venom potency varies by species. Symptoms appear more quickly if venom enters the bloodstream rapidly or if a high concentration of venom is injected.

How Afraid Should I Be?

Scorpions are generally shy and not aggressive. They will sting humans only if threatened, cornered or disturbed. Accidental human stinging occurs when scorpions are touched while in their hiding places, with most stings occurring on the hands and feet.

Even in the unlikely event that you are stung, scorpion stings are not serious problems, as no scorpions found in the Rocky Mountain region are particularly dangerous. While a sting might cause a temporary burning pain, most scorpion stings are no worse than a honeybee sting and they are rarely, if ever, fatal. It is important to note that there have been no reported deaths from a scorpion sting in the United States over the past 20 years.

The Arizona bark scorpion is the only potentially dangerous scorpion in the U.S., and it is generally found in southern Arizona, quite far from this region.

Preventing Scorpion Stings

- Never touch a scorpion. Scorpions are best left alone.

- Remove any debris around your house or camp that might hide scorpions, and avoid probing barehanded under lumber, rocks or other places that might hide a scorpion.

- Keep doors and windows of homes, tents and other shelters closed and caulk or repair any openings that scorpions might use to sneak in. Be sure to repair any torn screens and don't forget to check the dryer vent.

- Carefully inspect and handle firewood. It is best to wear leather gloves, long pants and shoes when working around potential scorpion hideouts.

- When camping in scorpion country, be sure to shake out shoes, gloves and clothing before you put them on in the morning. Scorpions are nocturnal.

- Avoid walking barefoot outdoors at night.

- Teach children about scorpions, and teach them to respect them, not fear them. Discourage them from playing around scorpion-infested areas.

- If you have an infestation in your home, contact a professional. For a non-toxic solution, consider dusting your attic with diatomaceous earth.

Treatment of Stings

- Keep the victim calm and quiet, and wash the area of the sting with soap and water.

- Pay attention to the victim's condition for the first 24 hours; be on the lookout for more serious symptoms such as throat swelling or difficulty breathing. If such symptoms occur, seek medical attention as soon as possible, as they may indicate an allergic reaction. If seeking medical attention, have someone carefully catch the scorpion. Make sure they take precautions to prevent a sting. Sweep the scorpion into a dustpan while wearing leather gloves. Then place the scorpion in a container in order to expedite identification, which can help with treatment.

- You can expect a reduction of redness and swelling within 48 hours. If you don't experience problems breathing, nervous system damage or a pronounced change in heart rate in the first 24 hours, the prognosis is good.

- Young children and the elderly are most susceptible to stings, and they might require assistance if stung. If a child exhibits symptoms of a scorpion sting, call the poison control center: it is open 24 hours a day, 7 days a week. **The "Poison Help" hotline number is 1-800-222-1222.**

- If necessary, apply a clean bandage to the wound.

- Place ice on the sting, or apply a cold, moist cloth to minimize swelling.

- Apply a hydrocortisone cream on the skin to reduce itching.

- Get a tetanus shot if it has been 5 years or more since your last one.

BOTTOM LINE

In this region, it's not likely you'll encounter a potentially dangerous scorpion. With that said, always be very cautious when probing in piles of lumber, brush or rocks or when you're around deserted buildings.

Bats

One of my earliest memories involves a bat. We were at my grandparents' house for Sunday supper. As the adults chatted while busily cleaning up after eating, I walked into the living room, bored for something to do. There on the floor in front of me was a small, round, furry object. I plunked myself next it. Unsure about what it was, I leaned over and blew on it. And in that moment, the serenity of Sunday was lost.

The bat lifted quietly into the air and flew erratically around the living room and dining room. Is it any wonder that I got scared when I heard the shrill screams from the kitchen and watched grown women shield themselves with dish towels?

Uh-oh, what had I awakened?!

About Bats

Like spiders, bats have been relegated to the halls of outcasts by virtue of the fact that they are as much the symbols of Halloween as Santa Claus is of Christmas.

Bats are the only true flying mammals. Flying squirrels can take to the air, but depend on gravity and the flap of skin that connects their legs to allow them to glide, not fly.

While there are approximately 950 species of bats in the world, there are only 29 species found in the Rocky Mountain region. With 27 species present in the state, New Mexico has the greatest number of species, while Idaho has 9 species of bats.

Life and Times . . .

Most bats in this region roost and bear their young in man-made structures, rocky crevices, under vegetation or underneath loose tree bark. Other bats in the region are solitary and live in the forest, roosting in the open.

hoary bat

Most of the bats in this region live on a diet of insects. However, some species feed on plant pollen and nectar and are important plant pollinators.

Bats in this region either migrate or hibernate during cooler months. Bats typically mate in the fall, prior to hibernation or migration, and they practice a strategy called delayed fertilization. Sperm from the male is stored in the female's uterus for up to 7 months; when the bats come out of hibernation or return from migration, the female ovulates (releases an egg from her ovary) and the stored sperm fertilize the egg. Mating requires time and energy and the practice of delayed fertilization helps conserve energy in the early spring, when food (insects) might be scarce.

When many migratory bats return in May, the females are pregnant. Most bats in this region have 1 offspring (called a pup) in June or July. Solitary bats, and those that roost in treetops, produce more offspring at a time, sometimes 2–4. The offspring of solitary bats are usually covered in thicker, more colorful fur than colony-dwelling bats, as they need the thicker fur to stay warm.

Colony-dwelling bats band together to stay warm, as the newborn, hairless pups are more likely to survive in a warm and humid place. The temperature in bat nurseries can climb to over 100 °F.

After the young are born, bat colonies become quite crowded. Researchers previously thought that adult females made no attempt to locate their own young within these masses, but nursed the first 2 pups they encountered upon their nightly return to the roost. Recent studies have shown that females actually recognize and feed their own young, which is a remarkable feat, given the confusion that must occur with such large swarms of bats.

Within a month, most of the young have fur, are nearly as large as adult bats and are capable of flying and feeding on their own. The adults soon leave, presumably migrating southward. Fledgling bats reside at the cave of their birth until the onset of cool weather in late fall drives them south.

Bats that hibernate are crowded, too; hibernation clusters can contain up to 300 bats per square foot! Hibernating dwellings must be cool but must stay above freezing. They also must be left alone; bats have a much better chance of surviving if they are not disturbed during hibernation. If they are disturbed, they burn the critical fat reserves needed to survive winter.

Fascinating Facts

- Amazingly, 1 out of every 5 mammal species in the world is a bat!

- As a bat flies in the night sky hunting for insects, it depends on echolocation to locate prey. The bat emits a pulse of very high-pitched squeaks, which is picked up by its oversized ears and used to determine the size and location of prey.

bat houses

- The echo does not travel far in air, so the bat can only make adjustments when it is within a few yards, hence the reason for its erratic flight.

Thanks to Bats

- Bats are prolific insect eaters capable of devouring 600–1,000 mosquitoes an hour! Many of the bugs they eat are pests to humans.

- Echolocation is remarkably similar to the active sonar used by modern antisubmarine system. Active sonar systems emit short bursts of sound; these sound waves bounce off any objects in the area and are reflected back. Bats process these echoes subconsciously; submarines use complicated computer systems and talented sonar operators to determine an object's location.

Myth Busters

MYTH: Bats are vicious carriers of rabies.

While some bats do transmit rabies, infected bats are rare.

MYTH: If you're not careful, a bat could get into your hair.

Not true. They certainly would not make a nest in the hair of such a dangerous creature. Thanks to echolocation, they can easily avoid foreign objects by swerving and weaving.

MYTH: Bats are filthy vermin!

While bat roosting areas often have a pile of dark, rice-sized droppings beneath them, the bats themselves always spend time cleaning and grooming themselves when they fly back to their roosts.

Why They Bite

When a bat feels threatened, its natural instinct is to flee or act defensively. The best defensive weapons they have are their tiny sharp teeth. While a bat bite is very rare, a bite by a rabid bat is even rarer.

How They Bite

As mammals, a bat's skeletal structure includes jaws and teeth. Bats have a unique pattern of teeth with a U-shaped gap separating the upper teeth; however, the dental equipment of these insect eaters is very small.

How Afraid Should I Be?

Get some sleep and don't worry about a bat biting you or your loved ones. You're far more likely to be in a car accident than be bitten by a rabid bat. In the United States, roughly 1 person dies each year from rabies due to a bat bite. Therefore, in a country with a population of approximately 300 million, your chances of being killed by a rabid bat are 1 in 300 million.

It's true that most of the human rabies cases in the Rocky Mountain region and the United States are caused by rabies-infected bats. However, more than 99 percent of bats are rabies-free. Generally, bats infected with rabies die quickly.

Preventing Bat Bites

- Do not handle live bats with your bare hands. This is especially true for sick bats—don't mess with them!

- You cannot get rabies simply from seeing a bat or touching its droppings, blood or urine. Touching a bat will not give you rabies unless the bat's saliva is transmitted through an open wound or via the mucous membranes of the nose, mouth or eyes.

- My preferred method of freeing a bat that somehow finds its way into our house is to sweep it into a butterfly net, just as if I were catching a butterfly. Easier said than done! Once the bat's in the net, I flip the net over so it can't get out. The entangled bat will likely be scared and displeased, and invariably will squeak and show its tiny set of sharp teeth. But I can casually walk the netted bat outside and flip it free.

- If I have to untangle the bat from the finely meshed net, I put on a pair of leather gloves that the bat's tiny teeth and weak jaws cannot penetrate.

- Keeping bats out of your home reduces the likelihood of a bite. Bats can enter through openings such as cracks, attic vents, rotted holes, loose screens and chimneys. They often choose attics and outbuildings because such spots are warmer and the crowded conditions are preferred bat nursery sites.

- Caulk or cover all potential openings into your home. Using poisons is not a good idea. The toxin could affect humans or pets, and could result in dead bats rotting in your walls.

- Erecting bat houses in your neighborhood also helps divert bats away from your home, while taking advantage of their natural insect control.

Treatment of Bites

- Treat a bat bite as you would a cat or dog bite. Wash the affected area and put an antiseptic on the wound before bandaging it. After taking care of the wound, it is best if you can capture the bat and immediately consult your local health department to have it tested for rabies. If you can't capture the bat, it's important to visit the doctor promptly for rabies vaccinations.

- Pets should have regularly scheduled rabies vaccinations. If you suspect a bat has bitten your unvaccinated pet, try to capture the offending bat and consult your veterinarian.

BOTTOM LINE

Seeing a bat flapping across the evening sky should be cause for celebration. Just think of all the mosquitoes and other bugs it's taking down! They are certainly not creatures to fear. Thanks to its sonar-like echolocation, it won't fly into your hair. And the chance of it biting you is extremely remote.

Rattlesnakes

Nothing motivates people as quickly as the one-syllable word "snake." When someone cries "SSSnake!" it will likely elicit an immediate, frightened response from others. The very word itself sounds a bit like a hiss. However, it's very unlikely that you'll be bitten by a venomous snake; you are far more likely to be hit by a car while walking or bicycling.

Even so, snakes are truly one of the premier outcasts in the animal world. Countless myths, untruths and tall tales are floating around out there that simply hang on for generation after generation. We fear snakes, so our children learn to fear snakes. However, by learning more about snakes we can understand their amazing adaptations—and hopefully even begin to admire them.

About Rattlesnakes

Rattlesnakes all belong to the genus *Crotalus*. The word is derived from the Greek *crotalon*, which translates to "little bell." The "little bell" refers to the rattlesnake's most famous characteristic—its rattle.

The only rattlesnake found throughout the entire Rocky Mountain region is the prairie rattlesnake (*Crotalus viridis*); it is also referred to as the western rattlesnake. There are 9 subspecies of the prairie or western rattlesnake. In the Rocky Mountain region, it is the most widespread venomous snake. (In comparison, the state of New Mexico alone is home to 7 rattlesnake species.) Even so, the likelihood of getting bitten by a prairie rattlesnake is very, very remote.

prairie   western diamondback   western massasauga

Life and Times . . .

Most of the rattlesnake subspecies in this region are named for the area they live in, and each region's subspecies vary in appearance. They often range in coloration from olive green to green-gray or a green-brown, and feature light-colored rings around the tail. These rings darken as the snake ages. Males generally have more rings than females.

All the rattlesnakes listed here have similarities; all rattlesnakes, large or small, have wedge-shaped heads that bear a pair of facial pits, elliptical-shaped pupils, and a tail tipped with the characteristic rattle. Rattlesnakes are primarily ambush feeders. They rely on camouflage to hide and wait for prey to pass within striking distance. Rattlesnakes primarily prey upon small rodents, shrews, frogs and ground-nesting birds. All species of rattlesnakes bear live young and usually produce a litter of 1–25. In this region, rattlesnakes usually bear young from August to October.

prairie rattlesnake

The most common rattlesnake in this region, the prairie/western rattlesnake can grow up to just over 5 feet in length. Its triangular head has a dark band that is sandwiched by 2 lighter-colored stripes; the dark band runs from the rear edge of the eye to the back of the jaw. Found in a variety of habitats, prairie rattlers can be found in everything from timberlines to scrub deserts, but they are often found on rocky slopes and in canyons. Prairie rattlers often frequent old mammal burrows and will sometimes overwinter with other rattlers in such dens. In the warmer, more southerly, part of the Rocky Mountain region, this snake prefers to move around at night.

Western diamondback rattlers are larger than the prairie rattlesnake; in fact, the western diamondback is the largest rattler in the Rocky Mountain region. It averages 4 feet in length but can reach lengths of 8 feet or more. In fact, the western diamondback is so large that it will often feed on cottontail rabbits. (It can take more than an hour for it to swallow such large prey.) However, the western diamondback is found only on the southern edge of the Rocky Mountain region in New Mexico; it prefers grassy plains, desert flats or rocky, forested areas.

The western diamondback has 2 dark stripes on its head, 1 on each side of its face; these stripes run diagonally, like Zorro's mask, from its eyes back to its jaws. Its tail is surrounded by alternating bands of light and dark, like the pattern of a raccoon's tail. When disturbed, the western diamondback will aggressively defend itself.

The smallest (and arguably the shyest) of the venomous snakes in this region is the western massasauga rattlesnake. This snake ranges from 18 to 40 inches in length and has 9 large scales on the top of its head. (The other rattler species mentioned here have many small scales on their heads.) The massasauga rattler is camouflaged and usually has a distinct line running backward from its eyes; this line often matches the blotchy coloration on its back.

While rattlesnakes have toxic venom, and bites can be very painful, they are rarely fatal to humans as they inject little venom into bites. Their first choice is to remain unseen by humans.

Fascinating Facts

- Like all snakes, rattlesnakes shed their skin approximately once a year. They leave behind their skin by literally crawling out of the skin that covers the scales. This is called ecdysis. Each time they shed their skin they acquire a new button or rattle on their tail. They shed their skin up to 5 times their first summer; after that, they shed only 1–3 times per summer.

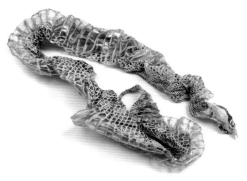

- The rattlesnake's loud, rapidly vibrating rattle is used to give a clear warning to anything seen as a threat to the snake.

shed rattlesnake skin

- All rattlesnakes are viviparous. That means that they do not lay eggs; their young are born alive.

- In the Rocky Mountain region, New Mexico has the most species of native snakes (46), while Montana has the least (10 species). There are roughly 140 species of snakes in United States and Canada.

- New Mexico is home to 7 species of rattlesnakes. Utah has 5, Colorado is home to 3 and Wyoming has 2 species of rattlesnakes. Montana and Idaho each have only 1 rattler species.

- In 1776, Colonel Christopher Gadsden presented the Continental Congress with a flag depicting a rattlesnake and the slogan "Don't Tread On Me," a direct warning to the British that, like the rattlesnake, the colonists would defend themselves fiercely if necessary.

Thanks to Rattlesnakes

- Rattlesnake venom has anticoagulant properties, and the potential medical applications of the venom have been extensively studied. The venom has been the subject of study for the treatment of arthritis, multiple sclerosis, strokes, heart attacks and polio.

- These snakes are quite beautiful and to see one (from a safe distance) is a thrilling and unforgettable experience.

- Rattlesnakes feed heavily on crop-damaging rodents. Plus, since snakes are members of a complex natural community, we have yet to discover all of their benefits.

Myth Busters

MYTH: All rattlesnake bites are venomous.

Approximately a quarter of all rattlesnake bites are dry bites, with no venom injected in the bite.

MYTH: Rattlesnakes will not strike in the dark.

Rattlesnakes can accurately strike, even in the dark. This is due to a pair of sensory pits located on both sides of the face, between the eye and the nostril. This characteristic is what lumps rattlesnakes into the group of snakes known as pit vipers. Keen heat-sensing cells located in the pit allow the snake to locate warm-blooded prey in the dark.

Why They Bite

Using toxic venom to kill prey is a brilliant survival strategy. The venom incapacitates the prey and the predatory snake can easily follow the dying creature and eat it without expending a lot of energy. The venom has a secondary benefit—for self-defense. Hence, the snake has venom for only 2 reasons: to secure food and to defend itself.

western diamondback

How They Bite

Any snake striking at you can be unnerving, but a rattlesnake bite is especially alarming. It happens in less than a second. Due to the fact that this is a venomous snake, it can kill you. But it is unlikely that it will.

The size of the rattlesnake, its age and health determine the potency and amount of venom that is delivered. Of the species covered here, the western diamondback is the largest, most aggressive and most dangerous.

A bite is nearly always preceded by rapid vibrating or rattling of the tail. This loud rattle serves as a clear warning to anything seen as a threat to the snake.

The bite itself is like a sudden, sharp, painful sting. The venom is injected by 2 specialized teeth called fangs. In some species, these teeth can measure nearly 1 inch long. The hollow canal inside the fang delivers the toxin from the venom supply to the tooth. The movable fangs resemble hypodermic needles and are capable of folding back in a sheath of membrane at the roof of the snake's mouth. When the snake strikes, the fangs extend forward to deliver the bite; even baby rattlesnakes have small fangs and are capable of injecting a small dose of venom. A snake sheds its fangs every 6–10 weeks.

THINK TWICE

For the most part, snakes are quite secretive and will try to avoid human contact. Think twice about trying to catch a rattlesnake just to show you can do it. And think twice about killing the snake. They do not go around looking for people to bite.

Think twice about getting close to a rattling snake for a photo. Even coiled, they are capable of striking from about one-third of their body length away.

The venom is a complex blend of chemical compounds. Many are proteins that are basically modified saliva enzymes, which help begin the process of digesting prey even before the snake swallows it. The venom attacks the nervous system, particularly nerves that are critical for breathing and blood flow. It can also attack red blood cells and tissues, causing bruising and internal bleeding.

How Afraid Should I Be?

Approximately 5 people die of snakebites (from rattlesnakes and other venomous snakes) in the United States each year. Bee stings and dog bites result in more human deaths. Still, if you suddenly come upon a venomous snake—or any snake for that matter—it might strike at you out of fear.

western massasauga

Metabolically, it is taxing for a snake to produce venom. Consequently, many snakes are thrifty in the use of their venom. Oftentimes the venomous rattlesnake bite contains little or no venom; these so-called dry bites occur in roughly 25–50 percent of all rattlesnake bites.

If you suddenly come upon a venomous snake, or any snake for that matter, it has no idea of your intent and it might strike at you out of fear. Though movies often depict encounters with writhing piles of snakes, snakes are generally solitary. Only during mating and hibernating periods do they occur in any numbers.

Preventing Rattlesnake Bites

- Rattlesnake bites can penetrate lightweight shoes and clothing. If you know you will be in thick foliage, you might want to wear knee-high leather boots.

- Practice caution when inspecting piles of lumber or other items that might provide a hideout for rattlesnakes. Use care around outbuildings where rodents live, as these areas are good hunting grounds for snakes. Avoid rocky outcroppings, particularly those facing south, where snakes might bask in the sun, particularly in early spring.

- If you see a rattlesnake, it will likely try to crawl away. Be sure to give it a lane of escape. If it feels trapped, it will typically coil and buzz its tail. Move slowly away from any unusual buzzing sound.

- If you know you will be in an area where rattlesnake encounters are common, you might want to purchase a venom pump extractor, which suctions the venom from the area of the bite.

Treatment of Bites

- If someone is bitten, move the person away from the snake and try to keep them calm. Lay the victim down with the bite slightly lower than the heart and keep them as still as possible. Remove all rings, bracelets or watches from the affected limb.

- Seek immediate medical help and get the victim to a medical facility as soon as possible. If possible, call ahead to warn the personnel (to be sure they have Wyeth Crotalidae Antivenin available).

- If you are alone and must go for help, go slowly so as not to exert yourself. With prompt treatment, death is unlikely.

- *Never* cut the snakebite, apply ice to the bite, suck the venom out with your mouth, or give any drugs or alcohol to the victim.

- The best snakebite kit includes a set of car keys, a cell phone and a companion.

BOTTOM LINE

It's very unlikely that you'll be bitten by a rattlesnake, as these snakes shy away from people. If you spot one, enjoy what may be a once-in-a-lifetime sighting and give the snake a wide berth as you leave the immediate area.

Other Snakes
Garter, Hognose, Gopher, Bull and Northern Water Snakes

As 12-year-olds, my buddy and I would flip over big pieces of scrap wood and sheet metal in hopes of finding a mess of garter snakes. When we saw one, we quickly grabbed it and stuffed it in a burlap sack. Of course, we occasionally got bitten. What would you do if some screeching giant pounced on you?

Worse yet, we'd take the writhing sack home to proudly show our catch to other family members—who we knew would get creeped out. We thought it was cool, but we were too young to know that we were reinforcing the universal fear and hatred for this innocent group of animals.

About these Snakes

In this region, New Mexico is home to 46 species of snakes, while Montana has only 10 snake species. There are roughly 140 species of snakes in United States and Canada. In the Rocky Mountain region, most snake species, venomous or not, will bite or threaten to bite you if you threaten or mishandle them.

For brevity's sake I will briefly cover 5 common nonvenomous snakes: garter snakes, hognose snakes (sometimes called blow snakes), gopher snakes, bull snakes and northern water snakes.

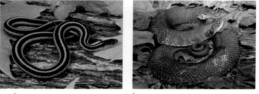

garter   hognose

gopher   bull   northern water

Life and Times . . .

COMMON GARTER SNAKE

This is the most common and widespread snake in North America. It is easily recognized by the 3 yellow stripes that run the length of its body. The background color is black or grayish brown.

Garter snakes will bite if confronted or captured. They thrash wildly when caught and often release their feces and a foul-smelling, musky spray that is potent and not easy to wash off.

hognose snake playing dead

HOGNOSE SNAKES

The western hognose snake is the most frightening-looking nonvenomous snake in our region; when it is threatened, it flattens out its head like a cobra, hisses loudly and often strikes . . . with a closed mouth.

A stout-bodied snake, the western hognose is lightly colored, usually tan or buffy gray. Its common name comes from its pronounced upturned, hoglike nose. If its seemingly aggressive behavior doesn't send you down the trail, it will roll on its back, open its mouth, hang its tongue out and do a fantastic job of playing dead. Its hope is that if it looks dead, you will leave it alone. Like the garter snake, it also has the ability to discharge a foul-smelling substance that might urge you to leave it alone.

GOPHER SNAKES

This is the longest snake in the Rocky Mountain region. Adults can measure up to 9 feet long! (The average size is around 4 feet in length.) The gopher snake's back is covered with dark brown blotches on a background color of yellow, tan or cream. A dark stripe on the head runs from the front of the eye to the angle of the jaw.

This open-country snake spends much of its time in semi-brushy areas, where it hunts burrowing underground mammals such as mice and gophers. It will also feed on some birds and bird eggs. Because it often hunts underground, it is not encountered very often.

When confronting a person, the snake will likely coil, buzz its tail and hiss very loudly. Because of this behavior, and because its coloration resembles that of a rattlesnake, it is often confused for a venomous snake and is unfortunately often killed by humans. A large adult gopher snake can deliver a painful bite if threatened.

BULL SNAKES

Bull snakes can reach impressive lengths. Adults can measure more than 6 feet long. This large snake is similar to the gopher snake, but its head is flecked in yellow with dark spots. Bullsnakes have a characteristic overbite, so their top jaw extends slightly more than the bottom jaw. Their snout is slightly more pointed than a gopher snake's.

This open-country snake spends much of its time underground, hunting burrowing mammals such as mice and gophers. Consequently, it is not encountered very often. When confronting a person, the snake will likely coil, buzz its tail and hiss very loudly. A large adult snake can deliver a painful bite.

NORTHERN WATER SNAKES

Northern water snakes are typically dark snakes with dark bands and blotches on a light brown or gray background. Older snakes look darker, and their bellies are white with reddish markings. Adults reach 2–4 feet long. As their name suggests, northern water snakes are found in wetlands.

When confronted, water snakes can have a nasty temper. They often flatten their heads, buzz their tails and strike, often repeatedly. Sometimes when they bite, they don't let go and bites can bleed freely because the snake's saliva contains an anticoagulant.

Fascinating Facts

- The common toad has a pair of glands on the back of its neck that can discharge a poison that makes it distasteful to most animals. The western hognose snake must think the poison is delicious; it loves eating toads!

- A breastbone, called the sternum, connects our ribs. Snakes do not have sternums. Their floating ribs allow them to move in a side-to-side motion and to swallow items larger than their own heads.

Thanks to Snakes

- They often feed on insects and small rodents that can be harmful to agricultural crops, and all snakes play an important role in the natural environment by contributing to ecological systems as predators and prey.

Myth Busters

MYTH: A snake's tongue is poisonous!

Not true. The tongue is a sensory organ used to detect smells. It picks up scent molecules and brushes them across a special organ on the roof of the mouth called a Jacobson's organ.

MYTH: Snakes are slimy!

This is a common misconception. Snakes are sometimes confused with amphibians, which have moist, slimy skin; at first glance, a snake's scales (and particularly the larger belly scales) are smooth and often shiny, making them appear wet. In reality, snakes and other reptiles have small dry scales.

Why They Bite

All of the snakes mentioned above will always try their best to avoid confrontations with humans. Flight and camouflage are their primary means of escape. However, if captured or cornered they often strike and bite.

How They Bite

None of these snakes have sharp fangs. Though their recurved teeth are sharp, they are quite small.

How Afraid Should I Be?

No need to be afraid. None of these snakes are venomous, and none have large teeth. Some of the larger snakes might break your skin with a bite, but the wound will be shallow and may

garter snake

not even bleed. With that said, if you or other family members handle reptiles, be aware that nearly all reptiles carry *Salmonella* bacteria and they often shed these bacteria in their feces. While these bacteria don't cause illness in snakes, *Salmonella* can cause serious illness in people. Most exposure results in diarrhea, fever and abdominal cramps. However, if it spreads to the bloodstream, bone marrow or nervous system, the infection can be serious and sometimes fatal. For the bacteria to spread to humans, fingers or objects that have been contaminated with reptile feces must be placed in the mouth. Thankfully, preventing *Salmonella* infection is easy. *Always* wash your hands with hot, soapy water after handling reptiles (snakes, lizards and turtles).

THINK TWICE

Think twice about picking up a snake. Unless you catch it properly and handle it gently, you might be bitten.

Preventing Snake Bites

- Don't crowd a snake. If you threaten it, it might bite.

Treatment of Bites

- It's okay to let out a "Yikes!"—but that is usually all you will have to do.

- If the bite breaks your skin, wash the wound and cover with a bandage if necessary. Watch it for the next few days for a secondary infection.

BOTTOM LINE

There is no need to be afraid. Snakes will do everything in their power to avoid you, and a bite from an undisturbed snake is very rare. Even if you manage to accidentally corner or upset one, these snakes are not venomous and don't have large teeth.

Skunks

Striped, Spotted, Hog-nosed and Hooded Skunks

It was mid-March and as we were driving back to Aunt Angeline's farm one evening, we had our car windows open a crack. In the darkness we came to a point where the unmistakable smell of the first skunk of the spring wafted into the car. Aunt Angeline inhaled deeply, and with great satisfaction she declared, "Ahh, there's nothing like a two-toned kitty with fluid drive!"

About Skunks

The Rocky Mountain region is home to 5 species of skunks. While striped skunks and eastern and western spotted skunks can be found across the entire region, hog-nosed skunks are limited to southern Colorado and New Mexico and hooded skunks are found only in New Mexico.

striped

western spotted

eastern spotted

hog-nosed

hooded

The striped skunk is the most common skunk species in the region; also known as a polecat, it has a V-shaped stripe that merges at the base of its head.

Spotted skunks are the smallest skunks found in the Rocky Mountains. Sometimes called civet cats or weasel skunks, 2 species of spotted skunks—the western and eastern—can be found in this region. The western spotted skunk is able to live in more arid conditions than other skunk species of this region, and not surprisingly, it has a wider range in this often dry region. Both species have a white spot on the forehead and varied stripes that run along the body. A spotted skunk's tail is only 6–8 inches long.

Hog-nosed skunks are found in Colorado and New Mexico. Also called rooter skunks, they are known for their habit of rooting up insects and grubs, and they have a white stripe and a white tail. These skunks prefer rocky denning sites. Not only do they winter in such dens, but they also use them as nurseries. Unlike the striped skunk, this species is more or less unsocial.

The hooded skunk has a very limited range in the United States, and is found only in parts of New Mexico. Hooded skunks get their name from the long fur on the upper neck. As they are nocturnal, they are rarely seen.

Life and Times . . .

If you want attention, make noise or dress wildly. In a world where most animals wear subdued colors so that they might better blend in with the countryside, skunks do not follow the rules. Their message is a loud and clear "HEY, LOOK AT ME! HERE I AM!"

These distinctly striped, black-and-white, cat-sized mammals are primarily nocturnal, so we rarely encounter them. When we do, it is usually in spring, summer and fall. During the winter months, they live in a den, sometimes sharing it with up to a dozen skunks. Such cuddling helps conserve energy. In the more moderate southern areas of the Rocky Mountain region, skunks can be active all year.

Skunks are most commonly found in farmland or semi-open areas. They tend to avoid forests. Active at night, they den up during the day in old woodchuck and badger burrows, and underneath rock piles, hollow trees or outbuildings. I remember discovering a skunk when a boyhood buddy and I flipped over an old car hood lying on the ground. We were looking for snakes but discovered a startled skunk!

All skunks are capable of delayed implantation—after mating, the fertilized egg remains dormant for months before it is implanted in the uterine wall and development of the embryo continues. For this reason, mating of the western spotted skunk often occurs in September or October, with implantation delayed until March. This

striped skunk

is the only time of the year when adult males and females are found together.

The female gives birth to 4–7 babies (kittens) from April to early June. The kittens stay with their mother for up to a year, though kittens are capable of breeding after 10 months.

hog-nosed skunk

Skunks are omnivores, feeding both on plants and animals. Like raccoons, they are quite opportunistic. They will feed on human garbage, bird eggs and even carrion. Since they often eat beetle grubs, ants and other underground insects, their front claws—longer than the back claws—are perfect tools for digging. Skunk diggings are common signs of their whereabouts.

Fascinating Facts

- Scientists long considered skunks a member of the weasel family (Mustelidae), but in 1997, a group of taxonomists determined that skunks were genetically very different from other Mustelidae members. For this reason, North American skunks and the related Asian stink badgers were put into their own separate weasel family called Mephitidae.

- Skunks have enough smelly liquid for 5 sprays. After that, it takes 10 days or so to produce more.

- The English word "skunk" is derived from the Algonquian Indian word *seganku*, meaning "one who squirts."

Thanks to Skunks

- Skunks, and especially young skunks, are a prey item for great horned owls, foxes, coyotes and bobcats.

- Skunks are an important component of the rich biodiversity of the Rocky Mountain region.

Myth Busters

MYTH: If your dog gets sprayed, give it a bath in tomato juice.

This old wives' tale has been around for some time. What really happens is that when your nose is subject to a high dose of skunk spray, you develop what is called olfactory fatigue. This means that your nose quits smelling the odor. Instead, you can easily smell the tomato juice and convince yourself that the skunk smell has been washed away. Someone coming upon the scene will gasp and tell you that the skunk smell is awful.

western spotted skunk

Why They Bite and Spray

When a skunk feels threatened, it will either lope away or lift its tail straight up, with all its tail hair erect to make the tail as noticeable as possible. The message is, "Watch it! Don't bother me!" A skunk also possesses 2 other defensive weapons—sharp teeth and a strong bite. While a skunk bite is very rare, a bite by a rabid skunk is even more uncommon.

How They Bite and Spray

Like other carnivorous mammals, skunks have 4 sharp canine teeth and scissorlike premolars called carnassials (last upper premolars and first lower molars). These teeth are adaptations dedicated to killing prey, and used to cut and tear meat. Clearly these same tools can be used as defensive weapons, and they are capable of delivering a nasty bite.

With such short, stubby legs, it isn't easy for a skunk to outrun a predator. The striped skunk has developed a unique defense system. When a skunk is threatened, it first tries to run away from the predator. If that doesn't work, it tries to frighten the attacker by arching its back, raising its tail and turning its back toward the threat. It may also stomp its feet. If this doesn't work, as a last resort, the skunk will spray the animal with a strong-smelling fluid. The fluid really stinks and can also sting the predator's eyes—giving the skunk time to get away. A skunk can spray as far as 15 feet!

Before spraying, the smaller spotted skunk will perform a comical-looking series of handstands while facing the intruder and fire directly over its own head.

THINK TWICE

Think twice about moving in to get the perfect photo of a skunk. If necessary, the skunk can spray its noxious delivery up to 15 feet!

Think twice when observing any skunk that is acting uncharacteristically bold. It could be harboring a disease or the rabies virus.

How Afraid Should I Be?

It is highly unlikely that you or your family will be faced with a skunk bite. A potentially dangerous skunk is one that becomes unafraid of humans. Normally these are shy, nonaggressive animals.

You should be suspicious of any skunk that is:

- Acting unusual, bold or aggressive

- Moving about during daylight hours

- Walking irregularly, almost as if it were drunk

If it displays one of these symptoms, there is a slight chance that it has rabies.

Non-Bite Concerns

Far and away the greatest fear in dealing with skunks is their chemical warfare weaponry. Being sprayed, or even being in the vicinity of a skunk spraying, is truly an unforgettable experience. Of course, the skunk is hoping that you will not forget it and perhaps next time you will give it a wide berth!

If a skunk sprays you, it can cause nausea and cause your eyes to burn. At the very least, you will likely find the encounter aromatically unpleasant!

striped skunk

The skunk's spray is a yellow oil composed of chemical compounds, called thiols, which contain sulfur. The foul concoction is stored in 2 prune-sized glands with openings in the skunk's anus.

Prior to spraying, the skunk will turn its rear end to face the threat (you!) and lift its plumelike tail straight up. The message at this point is a very clear "Okay, this is a warning! Back off!"

Preventing Skunk Bites or Sprays

- The best advice is to simply steer clear of wild skunks. Do not feed them or try to approach them. And if one tries to approach you or its tail stands up, move away!

Treatment of Bites and Sprays

- Treat a skunk bite as you would a cat or dog bite. If the wound is severe, seek medical attention. Since skunks are wild animals, you should contact the proper animal control agency and your doctor or the department of health for further advice. The offending animal should be tested for the rabies virus after biting a human.

- If you have been sprayed by a skunk, take off your clothes outside your home to prevent it from being "skunked." To remove skunk odor from your clothes or clean up towels, wash them with 1 cup of liquid laundry bleach per 1 gallon water.

- Take a very long, soapy shower!

- If your dog or cat has been sprayed, bathe the animal in a mixture of 1 quart of 3 percent hydrogen peroxide (purchase at a drug store), ¼ cup of baking soda (sodium bicarbonate) and 1 teaspoon of liquid detergent. After 5 minutes of bathing, rinse your pet with water and repeat bathing if necessary. Be careful to keep the solution out of the pet's eyes and mouth. To be effective, the mixture must be fresh, not stored. Note that the mixture might temporarily bleach your pet's hair.

- Products, such as Skunk-Off, are available for deodorizing pets. Carefully follow the directions, and keep in mind that none of these remedies work as well as time. Over the course of 2–3 weeks, the compounds in the spray will break down on their own.

BOTTOM LINE

It's highly unlikely that you or your family will be bitten by a skunk. Normally these are shy, nonaggressive animals. You are much more likely to be sprayed. While unpleasant, this is also a rare occurrence as long as you give skunks a wide berth—especially if one raises its tail!

Turtles

Snapping Turtles and Spiny Softshell Turtles

Snapping turtles have an image problem. Even their name, "snapping turtle,"
indicates aggressiveness. They are not cute. In fact, they are quite homely and their
nature is one of a grumpy old man. As youngsters, my friends and I used to spend
summers swimming in an abandoned gravel pit. A rarely seen, giant snapping turtle
we called "Old Moses" lived at the pit. This snapper became a legend and more
than once while swimming, one of my buddies would scream out, "It's Old Moses!
I felt him with my foot!!" Like junior Olympians we would race out of the water to
the security of dry land, where we would catch our breath, glad that we had escaped
with all of our toes. Little did we know that unprovoked snappers will not bite toes
while in the water.

About Turtles

Turtles have managed to survive on earth much longer than humans, and over millions of years they've adapted to live in almost any freshwater aquatic habitat, but in this region they are not found in mountainous areas. Instead, they prefer rivers, ponds and slow backwaters.

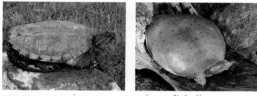

common snapping   spiny softshell

Snapping turtles are significantly larger than other turtles in the Rocky Mountain region. Snapping turtles have not been recorded in Idaho and are found only in the far southwest corner of Utah. In this region, 30–40 pound snappers are not uncommon, and giant specimens can weigh 50 pounds. Snappers are omnivores, and eat both plant and animal material. Excellent scavengers and stealthy hunters, they hunt by sitting still on the bottom of the wetland and ambushing their prey.

The Rocky Mountain region is home to another potentially aggressive turtle species—the spiny softshell turtle. Its range is limited; this species has not been recorded in Idaho and has been found only in the southwest corner of Utah.

Smaller than an adult snapping turtle, the softshell still can have a shell that measures 6–18 inches. Easily recognized by its rubbery, smooth shell and long, piglike nose, the softshell turtle is shy and uncommonly encountered. The profile of its shell is flat, and the shell is leathery and lacks the bony plates of most turtle species. The front edge of the adult turtle's shell is equipped with many small sharp spines.

The flat profile of the shell allows this turtle to deal with river currents as it flattens itself on the bottom of the river while hunting for minnows, crayfish and aquatic insects. Spiny softshell turtles prefer sandy or mud bottoms as opposed to rivers with rockier bottoms.

common snapping turtle hatchling

This turtle is very wary of humans and will quickly head underwater if encountered. The long neck, and slender, pointed snout serve as a snorkel, allowing it to breathe discreetly.

Like snapping turtles, softshell turtles are occasionally hooked by anglers. When frightened (e.g., when they are being pulled into a boat), they will likely try to bite. In such instances, it's often best to free the turtle by simply cutting the line.

Life and Times . . .

Snapping turtles mate at about 5 years of age. Once mating has occurred, the female snapping turtle heads to land and digs a hole with one of her back legs before depositing 25–50 round white eggs. This typically occurs in May or June. She covers the eggs with soil, and she then leaves. The warmth of the sun on the soil incubates them.

In roughly $2^1/_2$ months, the eggs hatch and the hatchling turtles must dig their way out of the nest. However, during cool summers, the eggs might remain in the ground and hatch the following spring. The hatchlings are never more vulnerable in their life than when they must make the dangerous (and often lengthy) journey from their birth nest to the water.

Fascinating Facts

- Since these turtles spend so much time in the water, their shells are often covered in green algae. Other species, such as painted turtles, bask in the sun more often, making it difficult for algae to grow.

- As with other turtle species, the temperature of the soil covering the buried eggs determines the sex of snapping turtles. Warmer soil temperatures tend to produce females.

- Snappers are capable of living for decades, much longer than most animals. The average lifespan of a snapping turtle is an estimated 30–40 years.

Thanks to Snapping Turtles

- Snapping turtles are important members of the cleanup crew in aquatic communities. Falsely accused of having a negative effect on fish populations, they actually help keep fisheries healthy by feeding on sick, injured or dead fish.

- Turtle eggs and hatchlings are often food items for raccoons, skunks, foxes, coyotes, herons and other predators.

Myth Busters

MYTH: The snapping turtle will bite off your finger or toe if it grabs you!

Though they make a lunging snap and an audible hiss, it is unlikely that one will sever any of your digits. Nevertheless, the larger the turtle and the more you struggle, the more likely you are to experience an open wound.

MYTH: During hibernation, snapping turtles can hold their breath all winter.

Snapping turtles and softshell turtles overwinter in hibernation on the bottom of wetlands. Without oxygen, they would die. They survive by slowing their

common snapping turtle

metabolism to the point where their biological systems are barely functioning. This requires very little oxygen, and they are able to absorb the little oxygen they need from the water itself. Most pond and lake water contains dissolved oxygen. The dissolved oxygen is absorbed directly through the turtle's thin skin, which is rich in a network of blood capillaries, found inside its mouth and around its rear end.

Why They Bite

Snapping turtles only bite when they feel threatened. Most bites occur when the turtle is out of the water.

How They Bite

As with other turtles, this reptile has no teeth. Instead, the turtle's mouth resembles a beak. Its sharp edges cut and shear food items ranging from crayfish and fish to salamanders, snails and plants. Therefore, a turtle bite is capable of cutting you. To defend itself, a snapping turtle will turn to face its attacker; be forewarned, it can extend its neck half the length of its upper shell!

How Afraid Should I Be?

This is one of those animals with a reputation bigger than its bite. In reality, this primitive reptile is not anywhere near the threat it is perceived to be. Turtle bites are extremely rare and they rarely happen in the water. However, a bite is likely on land—if you put yourself too close to the mouth of a frightened turtle.

Preventing Snapping Turtle Bites

- You can swim worry-free because they will *not* bite you in the water unless you are very careless and pose a threat to them. They will *not* pursue swimmers.

- When you encounter a snapping turtle out of the water, simply keep your distance and do not harass the turtle with sticks or other objects. Annoyed turtles are more likely to bite in their own defense.

common snapping turtle

Treatment of Bites

- If a turtle bites you and holds on, do not attempt to pull away. It will let go on its own. Admittedly, your first response is to pull away, but if you do, you increase the risk of the bite cutting you.

- Instead, try to stay calm, grit your teeth and patiently wait for the turtle to release its grip.

- If you receive a cut, wash it with clean water and soap, bandage it and seek medical attention if necessary.

BOTTOM LINE

Snapping turtles are nowhere near the threat people perceive them to be. Bites are extremely rare and only happen when a turtle feels threatened. Enjoy sightings of this prehistoric-looking animal from a respectful distance, and do not put yourself anywhere near its mouth. A snapping turtle can and will extend its neck half the length of its shell to defend itself.

Raccoons

"There is a beast they call aroughcun ["he who scratches with his hands"], much like a badger, but useth to live [in] trees as squirrels do. Their squirrels some are near as great as our smallest sort of wild rabbits, some blackish or black and white, but the most are gray."

—Captain John Smith, author of *Generall Historie of Virginia* (1624)

About Raccoons

There are more raccoons in the Rocky Mountain region today than there were 200 years ago. This adaptable mammal—which is famous for the distinctive black mask over its eyes and its fluffy, black-ringed tail—is both loved and scorned. Like a bandit, it can steal your heart or your picnic.

Though its long, sharp canine teeth clearly lump it into the mammalian order Carnivora, the raccoon is an omnivore that eats a broad range of foods and will not pass up an opportunity to fill its belly.

Its keen hearing, excellent night vision and amazing sense of touch are all adaptations for the nightlife it favors over daytime adventures.

Life and Times . . .

Raccoons prefer to live near trees and water. Though more common in stands of deciduous trees than in coniferous forests, this highly adaptable animal is comfortable living in both urban and wild environments. It is not unusual to find raccoons in abandoned houses or barns.

One reason this opportunistic mammal is so widespread is that it can eat a wide range of foods. An omnivore, it eats fruits, nuts, seeds, garden crops (such as corn and watermelons) as well as insects, bird eggs, crayfish, fish, frogs, small rodents, human trash and carrion (particularly roadkill).

In the Rocky Mountain region, male raccoons are slightly larger than females and begin to look for a mate in February, with mating peaking in March. Raccoons are capable of breeding all spring and into summer. After roughly 65 days of pregnancy, the female gives birth to 2–6 young.

After a month or so, the young leave their birthing den and join the mother in foraging for food. They will stay with their mother through their first winter before heading out on their own the following spring. One-year-old females are capable of breeding and producing young.

In the colder parts of this region, raccoons are said to "hibernate" during periods of inclement weather. Not true hibernators, they do become dormant and will often share denning quarters. This cuddling behavior conserves heat and helps them survive cold weather.

Fascinating Facts

- Related to coatis and ringtails, the raccoon is the only member of the Procyonidae family found in the Rocky Mountain region. (*Procyon* is Latin for "before dogs." This refers to the fact that the raccoon's ancestors have been around longer than those of dogs and wolves.)

- Some Native Americans refer to the raccoon as the "bear's little brother." Like a bear, it walks on all 4 feet with an arch in its back, and has claws that don't retract. And like humans and bears, the raccoon walks using the entire sole of the foot "heel to toe."

- Their clawed feet, each bearing 5 toes, help make them excellent tree climbers. Their reasonably long tail serves as an aid in balance.

Thanks to Raccoons

- Raccoon fur has been harvested for clothing for centuries.

- Raccoons are a food item for other wildlife such as coyotes. They are also a food source for some people.

- They are an important component to the rich biodiversity of the Rocky Mountain region.

Myth Busters

MYTH: Raccoons always wash their food before eating it.

While this might be good advice for us, it is not the case with raccoons. Their species name *lotor* means "washer," but raccoons do not always dunk their food, even when near water, and will not hesitate to eat when water is not nearby. Biologists are unsure as to why raccoons have this strange habit.

Why They Bite

When threatened, the raccoon's natural instinct is to flee or act defensively. Its best defensive weapons are its sharp teeth and strong bite. While a raccoon bite is very rare, a bite by a rabid raccoon is even rarer.

How They Bite

Like other carnivorous mammals, raccoons have 4 sharp canine teeth and scissorlike shearing premolars called carnassial teeth (last upper premolars and first lower molars). These are adaptations for killing prey, and for cutting and tearing meat. Clearly they can also be used as defensive weapons. Given the raccoon's speed, its relatively strong jaws and sharp teeth, it is capable of delivering a nasty bite.

THINK TWICE

Think twice about keeping a baby raccoon for a pet. In fact, it may be illegal for you to keep one as a pet without a proper permit.

Think twice about feeding a raccoon. Putting your hand in front of any wild animal's mouth is never a good idea. A seemingly harmless situation could turn into a bite delivered by the nervous raccoon.

How Afraid Should I Be?

It is unlikely that you or a member of your family will be bitten by a raccoon. A potentially dangerous raccoon is one that becomes unafraid of humans. Normally these are shy, nonaggressive animals. You should be suspicious of any raccoon that is acting boldly or aggressively. There is a slight chance that it is infected with rabies.

Non-Bite Concerns

RABIES

Only mammals are affected by the rabies virus, which is carried in saliva. Rabies is a serious infection of the nervous system. If not treated quickly, it is capable of making a person very ill and death almost always results.

Rabies is occasionally found in raccoons. In the United States, more than 7,000 animals (wild and domestic) are diagnosed with rabies annually. It is usually transmitted by a bite. Though non-bite infections are rare, it is possible for infected saliva to enter the eyes, nose, mouth or an open wound.

Avoid contact with any raccoon that displays unusual, bold or sickly behavior. Animals that have rabies are often described as "foaming at the mouth." This happens because the animal's nerves no longer work properly and it can't swallow its own saliva. If you find a dead raccoon, do not handle it with bare hands. For more on rabies, see pp. 10–11.

RACCOON ROUNDWORM (*BAYLISASCARIS PROCYONIS*)

Though it is not the result of a bite, a roundworm found in the feces of some raccoons can cause misery in humans. Raccoons are the primary host of this roundworm, which is commonly found in their small intestines. If it infects a human, the microscopic, migrating roundworms can cause skin irritations, as well as eye and brain damage. There have been few human deaths, all of them in children, but one should be aware of the possibility of transmission nonetheless.

Raccoon feces can carry millions of roundworm eggs. Humans can encounter the eggs through contact with raccoon droppings or by touching a contaminated area or object (the eggs persist long after the feces disappear). Small children are especially vulnerable because they often put their fingers, objects or even droppings into their mouth. Any area contaminated with raccoon feces should be cleaned and the feces should be burned, along with any affected feed, straw, hay or other materials. Raccoons are also hosts for leptospirosis and giardiasis, both of which can be a health concern for humans.

Preventing Raccoon Bites and Roundworm

- The best advice is to not approach wild raccoons or allow them to approach you.

- The best way to prevent a roundworm infection is to minimize contact with any area inhabited by raccoons. Roundworm eggs are very resistant to environmental conditions and can survive for several years. Children and pets should be kept away from these contaminated areas until a thorough cleaning has occurred. It is important to keep decks and picnicking areas around your home clean of food scraps, as these might attract raccoons.

Treatment of Bites

- Treat a raccoon bite as you would a cat or dog bite. Wash the wound, stop the bleeding with a compress, bandage it and seek medical attention. Since it is a wild animal, you should contact the proper animal control agency and your doctor or the department of health for further advice.

- After receiving medical care, monitor the bite for a possible infection.

- Rabies is treatable through a series of vaccinations. Every year approximately 40,000 people in the United States receive these shots as a precaution.

- Roundworm treatment is very difficult. If someone's been exposed, or even suspects exposure to raccoon roundworm, seek immediate medical care. There are currently no drugs that can effectively kill the larvae moving in the body. Laser surgery has been successfully performed to kill larvae present in the retina of the eye, but the damage caused by the migrating larvae is irreversible. Treatment with steroids in intermediate hosts is mainly supportive and is designed to decrease the inflammatory reaction.

- Getting a tetanus shot is a good idea.

BOTTOM LINE

It's unlikely that you or a member of your family will be bitten by a raccoon. Still, a raccoon that is sick, injured or has become unafraid of humans is a potentially dangerous animal. Reduce your risk by not approaching raccoons or allowing them to approach you—especially ones that are acting boldly or aggressively.

Coyotes

A long, long time ago, people did not yet inhabit the earth. A monster walked upon the land, eating all the animals—except Coyote.

Realizing that Coyote was sly and clever, the monster thought of a new plan. It would befriend Coyote and invite him to stay in its home. Before the visit began, Coyote said that he wanted to visit his friends and asked if he could enter the monster's stomach to see them. The monster allowed this, and Coyote cut out its heart and set fire to its insides. His friends were freed.

—Nez Perce Indian story called "Coyote and Monster"

About Coyotes

Among many American Indian tribes, coyotes hold a special place in oral storytelling. Taking the role of trickster, the coyote is considered a very special animal.

Though coyotes originally branched out from the open grasslands and deserts of the southwestern United States, they have spread all across North America. They are common across the Rocky Mountain region. Extremely adaptable, these highly social animals often live within city limits. More and more local jurisdictions are adopting coyote control ordinances.

Life and Times . . .

These wild members of the dog family are highly social animals. They are most active at dawn and dusk, though it is not unusual to hear family groups yapping and howling throughout the evening. This does not mean that they are making a kill; it could simply be a means of "singing" and reinforcing their family unit.

Despite their preference for hunting during low-light periods, they can be seen at any time of the day. If you spot one, there is a good chance that others are nearby.

Resembling a small German shepherd with sharp, pointed ears, the average coyote weighs 20–40 pounds. The muzzle is slender and narrow, more like a fox than a wolf. When a coyote runs, its black-tipped tail droops below its back. Dogs and wolves typically run with their tails level to upright.

A coyote pair may stay together for life. The female comes into her estrus cycle (comes into heat) once a year, sometime from January into March, and mating occurs over a period of 4–5 days. The pups, averaging 5–7 per litter, are born about 2 months later in an underground den.

One reason coyotes are so widespread is that they can eat almost anything and cope quite well with humans. They can be found in almost any habitat. Wild foods include small rodents, rabbits, hares, squirrels, birds, insects, fruits, reptiles, amphibians and occasionally deer (usually road-killed, crippled or sick deer). Non-wild foods include garden produce, domestic cats, dogs, small livestock and abundant human garbage.

Humans have removed most of the coyote's traditional predators, which included grizzly and black bears, mountain lions and wolves. The numbers of some of these species are rebounding, but only in localized areas, and such population booms aren't widespread. While humans have unknowingly played a major role in the success and spread of coyotes, we are also their major enemy.

Fascinating Facts

- Coyotes occasionally mate with domestic dogs. Their young are referred to as coydogs. Coydogs generally do not make good pets, however, as they are more nervous than dogs and therefore more likely to bite.

- Coyotes can actually run faster than a roadrunner! They can run 40 miles per hour and leap an 8-foot fence.

- Like your pet dog, coyotes maintain their territories by scent marking (peeing along boundaries), howling and barking.

- The scientific name for the coyote, *Canis latrans*, means "barking dog." Coyotes communicate through howling, yelping, barking and huffing. Howling is used to communicate with other coyotes in the area. It is generally used to declare territorial rights. It is also an invitation for females to join the howling male. Yelping sounds wildly exuberant, and it is a form of celebration for an assembled pack; it is also heard in play. Barking is usually a threat display when a coyote is possessing a kill or guarding its den. Huffing is a call rarely heard by humans; it is usually softly delivered to call coyote pups without drawing the attention of nearby predators such as wolves or humans.

THINK TWICE

Think twice if you're tempted to feed a coyote. By feeding it you are reinforcing behavior that will create a nuisance animal and likely shorten its life. And you are increasing the odds of being bitten.

Thanks to Coyotes

- The fur of coyotes has been harvested for clothing for thousands of years.

- Coyotes feed heavily on many small rodents, squirrels and woodchucks, which are sometimes pests to agricultural crops.

- They are an important component of the rich biodiversity of the Rocky Mountain region.

Myth Busters

MYTH: Coyotes that are out in the daytime are likely rabid.

Although it could be rabid, it is not likely. More than likely it is a healthy coyote that's feeding more than usual, particularly if there are young pups to feed.

MYTH: Coyotes kill mostly game animals, making them the primary competitor of game-hunting humans.

This is a highly contentious issue in the Rocky Mountain region. There are many who believe that coyotes have a negative impact on game, particularly deer populations. The controversy has put wildlife advocates at odds with those who want coyotes removed and highlights the divisiveness the coyote has brought to communities across the region. Research shows that coyotes in both urban and rural areas feed primarily on rodents. However, if given the opportunity, they will not turn down a white-tailed deer fawn or a clutch of pheasant eggs. And as Canada geese have flourished, some coyotes have learned to flush geese off their nests and steal the eggs.

Why They Bite

While thousands of dog bites are treated each year in the Rocky Mountain region, coyote bites are extremely rare. The natural instinct for a coyote that feels threatened is to flee or act defensively. Its best defensive weapons are its sharp teeth and bite. While a coyote bite is very rare, a bite by a rabid coyote is even less common.

Animals that have become habituated to humans deliver almost all coyote bites. Often found around campgrounds and picnic areas, these coyotes should not be trusted.

How They Bite

Like other carnivorous mammals, coyotes have 4 sharp canine teeth and scissorlike shearing premolars called carnassials (the last upper premolars and the first lower molars).

These are adaptations for killing prey and cutting and tearing meat, but they can also be used in self-defense. With their speed, relatively strong jaws and sharp teeth, coyotes are capable of delivering a nasty bite.

How Afraid Should I Be?

It is unlikely that you or your family will be bitten by a coyote. A potentially dangerous coyote is one that becomes unafraid of humans. Normally these are shy, secretive animals. Most coyote bites happen in areas where they have become habituated to humans—particularly where humans are feeding them. Records of coyote attacks on humans show that when attacks do happen, children under the age of 5 are typically the likeliest to be attacked. You should be suspicious of any coyote that is acting boldly or aggressively.

RABIES

In the Rocky Mountain region, the coyote is rarely a rabies carrier. Bats, skunks and raccoons have a higher incidence of harboring rabies. For more information on rabies risks and precautions, see pp. 10–11.

Preventing Coyote Bites

- Never approach or attempt to touch a coyote.

- Discourage coyotes from hanging around your home. Uneaten food attracts unwanted visitors, including coyotes. Keep food garbage cleaned up. Make composted foods unavailable through proper screening, or place them in an enclosed composter.

- Keep small to midsize pets indoors, and if you feed larger pets outdoors, be sure that all uneaten food is cleaned up.

Treatment of Bites

- If you are bitten by a coyote, wash the wound, stop the bleeding with a compress, bandage it and seek medical attention. Since a coyote is a wild animal, you should contact the proper animal control agency and your doctor or the department of health for further advice.

- Puncture wounds should be thoroughly flushed and cleaned with a topical antibiotic. Deep puncture wounds require medical assistance.

- Watch for possible infection.

BOTTOM LINE

Most coyotes avoid humans, and attacks are extremely rare. The few bites reported have nearly always involved animals that have grown comfortable around humans and are unafraid of them. Coyotes hanging around campgrounds and picnic areas where ill-advised feeding occurs should not be trusted.

Gray Wolves

If you were assigned to brand or market the idea of wilderness, you would likely consider the gray wolf as one of its symbols. Ironically, in the Rocky Mountain region wolves are proving to be very adaptable and more live outside the backcountry wilderness regions than within it.

For centuries, humans have had a love-hate relationship with the gray wolf. Native Americans considered the animal a sign of strength, cunning and a good provider, while early European settlers considered the wolf a threat to the opening of the wilderness. In 1914, the United States Congress even approved funding to kill wolves, reducing the population significantly. Thanks to protection and recovery efforts, there are now approximately 5,000–6,000 wolves in the United States, excluding Alaska.

About Gray Wolves

Prior to 1986, there were a few remnant packs of wild wolves in the northern Rocky Mountains. The U.S. Fish and Wildlife Service designated 3 separate wolf recovery areas in the northern Rockies: northwest Montana, central Idaho and the Yellowstone National Park area. In the mid-1990s, approximately 76 wolves were introduced to Yellowstone National Park and central Idaho. According to 2009 records, the northern Rockies wolf population stands at 1,706 wolves in 242 packs and 115 breeding pairs. And now breeding pairs have been confirmed in eastern Washington and Oregon. The goal of the recovery effort is to remove wolves from the endangered species list (delist) after certain population objectives have been met; so far, the wolf's recovery has been a major success story, as this species has been reintroduced into portions of its former range.

Life and Times . . .

The gray wolf is the largest member of the wild dog family in North America. Weighing up to 130 pounds, it is typically much larger than a coyote, with longer legs (but shorter ears).

Male wolves are slightly larger than females. Both are highly social animals and live in packs. The pack is made up of the breeding pair (known as the alpha pair), their pups and other nonbreeding adult wolves. A wolf's ability to survive depends on the strength of the pack. Not only are they a family unit, but they also cooperate to hunt, raise young and defend their territory (50–1,000 square miles) from other packs and individual wolves.

A pack of 6–8 wolves typically kill about 1 deer per day, or 1 elk every 3 days, or 1 moose every 4–5 days. They can survive eating about $2^1/_2$ pounds of food per wolf per day. To reproduce successfully they need slightly more than double that amount.

Capable of breeding at 2–3 years, gray wolves sometimes mate for life. After breeding in January and February, an average of 5 pups are born in early spring. Like other mammals, the pups depend on their mother's milk for the first part of their lives. After weaning, the pups are fed regurgitated meat brought back by members of the pack. At about 8 months, the young wolves are running and hunting with the adults. As carnivores, they eat a range of animals, including deer, moose, elk, beavers, hares, mice and assorted other small mammals.

Fascinating Facts

- When hunting, wolves might travel 30 miles in a day. They trot along at 5 miles per hour but can sprint up to 40 miles per hour.

- Why do wolves howl? Biologists have learned that wolves howl not to simply communicate. Sometimes they simply like to howl—kind of like singing in the shower! Howling also reinforces pack unity and harmony. It might announce the start or end of a hunt, or sound a warning to other wolves, including those in their own pack, as well as wolves from neighboring packs.

Thanks to Gray Wolves

- Besides being a prominent symbol of the wilderness, these amazing creatures have long been admired by humans, and we enjoy hearing their howls, watching them in the wild and photographing them.

Myth Busters

MYTH: You never want to be in the woods with a wolf pack nearby!

For hundreds of years the wolf has been persecuted and perceived to be dangerous. In fact, there has only been 1 documented incident in North America where a human was killed by wolves, and there have been no documented wolf attacks on humans in the Rocky Mountain region.

Why They Bite

Wolves will usually go out of their way to avoid humans and are rarely a threat. Most reported attacks on humans involved wolves that had been fed by people and had become habituated. Wolves are wild animals and should be treated as such.

How They Bite

Like other carnivorous mammals, wolves have 4 sharp canine teeth and scissorlike shearing premolars called carnassials. These are adaptations for killing prey and tearing food, but they work well as defensive weapons.

How Afraid Should I Be?

There is no need to be afraid. Despite the recovery of the wolf population, there have been no documented attacks on humans in the Rocky Mountain region. If you see a wild wolf, consider yourself lucky, as they are still quite rare.

THINK TWICE

Think twice if you see a wolf that is unafraid of humans. A normal wolf should be very afraid of a human. If you see such unusual behavior, contact the US Fish and Wildlife Service.

Preventing Gray Wolf Bites

• Never approach or attempt to touch a wolf.

• To discourage wolves from hanging around your home, keep small pets indoors. If you feed pets outdoors, be sure that all uneaten food is put away. Keep garbage cleaned up, and make sure composted foods are inaccessible.

Treatment of Bites

• If you are bitten by a wolf, contact the proper animal control agency and if it's not a serious wound, treat it as you would a cat or dog bite. Puncture wounds should be thoroughly flushed and cleaned with a topical antibiotic. Deep punctures and other serious wounds require assistance.

• Watch for possible infection of the bite site.

BOTTOM LINE

Wolves will go out of their way to avoid humans. Your chance of even seeing a wolf in the Rocky Mountain region is very slim. Consider yourself very lucky if you spot one.

Cougars

I'd been trout fishing the Price River when I saw several hundred yards ahead on the railroad grade something that looked like a big chow dog. I ignored it and went down to the stream to continue fishing. Wondering where the dog went, I climbed back up the railroad grade. There, 75 feet from me (I measured later) stood the biggest mountain lion I have ever seen. Its ears went down, but the tail did not move. I wondered if it was considering me a meal. I silently waved both arms, fly rod in hand, and jumped up and down. The cat leaped into the air. I thought, "This is it." But in midair it turned, jumped off the grade and in 3 bounds, the cat, in total silence, was gone.

—shared by a good friend who lives in Utah

About Cougars

This large cat has many names; these include cougar, puma, mountain lion, catamount and painter. It is best identified by its thick, long, brown tail that is tipped with darker hair. These predators are larger than a German shepherd dog and generally weigh 80–200 pounds.

The cougar's stronghold is the Rocky Mountain region, though it has been expanding its range across North America. Wildlife biologists estimate that there are currently approximately 80,000 cougars in the western United States.

In areas with farms and rangeland, the hunting habits of cougars can put them in conflict with humans because of occasional livestock predation.

Life and Times . . .

The largest cat in North America, and the fourth-largest cat species in the world, cougars are remarkably stealthy predators.

Usually these cats are residents or an area or they are passing through an area. Transient cougars are usually young animals that have recently left their mother or older animals that have left familiar territory. Cougars will scent mark the edges of their territory by scratching the ground with their claws.

Cougars live, hunt and travel alone except during the mating season or when females have young kittens. When these kittens begin to disperse, they sometimes remain with each other for a while.

Female cougars generally mate at around 2 years of age. The males don't sexually develop until they are $2^{1}/_{2}$–3 years old. This reduces the likelihood of a brother and sister mating with each other, which would weaken genetic viability.

Like domestic cats, when the female comes into heat (estrus) she is very vocal and yowls and screams loudly. She is in heat for approximately 7 days. After attracting the larger male, they will stay together for several days mating up to 9 times per hour.

Dominant male cougars will kill other males, as well as cougar kittens. They generally cover a larger range than females, sometimes up to 22 square miles.

After a gestation of roughly 3 months, the female will retire to a cave, a rocky overhang or a similar hideout and give birth to 1–6 kittens during the summer

months. Kittens are born with a spotted coat, which disappears in 6–9 months. The youngsters stay with their mother for 2 years and during that period the mother will not mate. If the kittens die, the female will shortly come into estrus (heat) and breed again.

As carnivores, they generally kill their own food using stealth and an amazing burst of speed. Favorite prey includes deer, elk, antelope, rabbits, hares, wild turkeys, raccoons, squirrels, mice, assorted other small mammals and even fish. These shy predators hunt primarily at night, though they have been observed at all times of the day. After making a kill and eating their fill, cougars generally rake sticks, leaves or needles over the carcass, in order to hide it so they can return to feed on it later.

Cougar populations often correspond with prey density and the population levels of deer and elk in the area. Other factors that affect cougar populations include landscape changes (such as wildfires), pressure from human population and development, and competition with other predators such as wolves.

Fascinating Facts

- An elk kill provides a cougar with enough food for 3 weeks, while a cougar can subsist on a deer for 2–5 days. While a male cougar might kill and feed on 20 deer per year, a female with kittens to feed might feed on 40 deer.

- Cougars are found from Central America to the Yukon Territory in northern Canada and from the Atlantic Ocean to the Pacific Ocean. Among large mammals, only humans range more widely.

Thanks to Cougars

- Besides being a prominent symbol of the wilderness, these amazing mammals are always a popular species of wildlife for humans to watch and photograph.

- They are an important component to the rich biodiversity of the Rocky Mountain region and a key player in predator-prey relationships.

Myth Busters

MYTH: Cougars will attack people if the conditions are right (or wrong).

Less than 1 percent of cougars will "lock on" to humans as potential prey. And these animals usually have some physical problem or illness that makes them inefficient hunters.

MYTH: Cougars will leap from trees on their prey.

While cougars are extremely stealthy, they depend primarily on their ability to stalk and pursue with a burst of speed . . . all from the ground.

Why They Bite

Cougars will usually go out of their way to avoid humans. But there are instances when cougars have preyed on humans. Most reported attacks on humans are predatory; they are seeking food.

How They Bite and Claw

Cougars usually move rapidly toward their prey with a burst of speed before leaping on the prey's back. They then bite down on the neck of their prey and sever the spine. On larger animals they sometimes reach around the snout of the animal, pulling its head back and breaking its neck.

Like other carnivorous mammals, cougars have 4 sharp canine teeth and scissor-like shearing premolars called carnassials (last upper premolars and first lower molars). These are adaptations for killing prey and cutting and tearing food, but they work well as defensive weapons. With their quickness, exceptionally strong jaws and sharp teeth, cougars are capable of inflicting a serious bite.

Like other cats, cougars also have very sharp claws. Unlike canines, which have fixed claws, a cougar's claws are retractable. In other words, the claws are hidden until the cat's paw is stretched out. When the paw relaxes, the tendon in the foot relaxes and the claw is pulled in. The sharp claws allow the cat to easily climb trees and they are useful in attacking prey.

How Afraid Should I Be?

While it is true that cougars will kill livestock, pets and even humans, it's unlikely that you'll see one in the wild, let alone be attacked by one. Over the past 120 years there have been 21 documented human deaths as a result of cougar attacks, with 11 since 1990. Biologists feel that this increase is due to a couple factors. First, the total human population has increased, and there has been a subsequent increase in the amount of people spending time hiking, mountain biking, backpacking, fishing, hunting, and running in cougar habitat. Second, in many areas of cougar habitat there has been an increase in prey animals, particularly deer, leading to a rise in the cougar population.

THINK TWICE

Think twice if you see a cougar that is unafraid of humans. A normal cougar should be very afraid of a human. If you see such unusual behavior, contact the U.S. Fish and Wildlife Service.

To put your chances of being attacked by a cougar in perspective, consider this: approximately 115 people die every day in vehicle crashes in the United States. That is roughly 1 death every 13 minutes. And yet we don't cower in fear each time we get into a car, but many people are instinctively (and perhaps irrationally) afraid of cougars and other wild animals.

Preventing Cougar Bites and Scratches

- Never approach or attempt to touch a cougar.

- Discourage cougars from hanging around your home or cabin by keeping pets indoors, keeping pet food indoors and being sure that all uneaten pet food is cleaned up.

- Keep children close to you when in cougar habitat. If a cougar is sighted, be sure to place yourself between the cougar and the child. NEVER tell the child to run to you. The cougar might be triggered to pursue the fleeing "prey."

- If you see a cougar, don't run or turn your back. It's hardwired to chase fleeing prey animals.

- Stand up tall, and if necessary, raise your arms high. You want to look as big and imposing as possible. Be aggressive. Yell, shout, throw rocks or sticks toward the cougar. If attacked, do not relax and play dead. Be aggressive and fight with whatever is at hand—a club, stick, rock, hiking stick or even your bare hands. Move slowly away and leave the area or seek shelter. At night, use a bright flashlight to scare a cougar away.

Treatment of Bites and Scratches

- If you are bitten or clawed by a cougar, contact a doctor immediately and the local department of health. Also be sure to contact the U.S. Fish and Wildlife Service to inform them a cougar attack has occurred in the area.

- If it's not a serious wound, treat it as you would a dog or cat bite. Puncture wounds or scratch injuries should be flushed and thoroughly cleansed with a topical antibiotic. Deep punctures, gashes and other serious wounds require medical assistance.

- Watch for possible infection of the bite.

BOTTOM LINE

Cougars usually go out of their way to avoid humans. It's unlikely that you'll even see a cougar in the Rocky Mountain region. Consider yourself very lucky if you see one.

Bears

Black Bears and Grizzly Bears

Among indigenous cultures, few wild animals have held such a place of honor as the black bear. They were held sacred, and to be offered Bear Medicine was a highly revered gift. Perhaps we need to keep in mind the American Indian concept of Bear Medicine—to practice introspection and take in all the facts, give it critical thought and then act.

I had not originally intended to include the black bear in this book. However, when I surveyed outdoor professionals and enthusiasts about which creatures to cover, the black bear kept popping up as an animal that strikes fear into the hearts of many folks. You know the familiar mantra, "Lions and tigers and bears. Oh my!" We have grown up with this fear constantly being taught to us.

About Black Bears and Grizzly Bears

Black bears and grizzly bears are native to the Rocky Mountain region. Between the 2 species, the black bear is far more widespread and common. It is likely that the entire population of grizzly bears found in the Lower 48 live in the Rocky Mountain region.

black bear

There are several primary physical differences between these species of bears. Grizzly bears are typically larger than black bears and have a distinct profile, as they have a shoulder hump. They have a more compact, dished face and their ears are less prominent than in black bears. Coloration isn't always the best way to identify a bear, as black bears are oftentimes brown in color.

grizzly bear

Bears are omnivores, and these opportunistic feeders feed on a wide variety of foods, including plant foliage, berries, fruits, roots, fish, insects, small mammals and sometimes young ungulates (hoofed animals such as deer, elk and antelope). According to bear studies in British Columbia, plants make up 90 percent of their diet. When presented with the opportunity, they also feed on human garbage, birdseed and, yes, even camp food.

As the black bear population grows, more people are seeing these magnificent beasts. Yet the greatest threat to bears is loss of habitat. As humans continue to build homes and cabins in bear country, the likelihood of encounters with bears is greater. Unfortunately, any bear that shows up looking for food is considered a nuisance or a threat and such bears are often shot.

Life and Times . . .

These specialized hibernators usually den up for winter in October and November. Grizzly bears usually hibernate at higher elevations.

Unlike some mammal hibernators such as the woodchuck or ground squirrel, a bear's winter body temperature does not change dramatically from its summer body temperature. During the winter months, a female bear gives birth to 2–3 cubs. Each cub weighs less than 1 pound at birth. She is able to nurse the bears on high-fat milk that she produces from her stores of body fat. The cubs generally stay with their mother for 2 winters before going off on their own.

grizzly bear

By the end of March and early April, the bears are on the move and begin looking for food. Their mating season takes place in early summer around the month of June. The bear's primary job in summer and early fall is to eat; during these seasons they must consume 1 year's worth of food in 6 months.

Fascinating Facts

- The black bear is the most widespread of the 3 North American bear species. The other two are the grizzly bear (also called the brown bear) and the polar bear.

- While an adult human might consume an average of 1,500 calories per day, the black bear can consume 30,000 calories per day when readying itself for hibernation!

- Bears and dogs are close relatives. Taxonomists believe that they share a common ancestor.

- Grizzly bears likely evolved in wide-open areas, such on as plains or on the tundra. Black bears evolved in forests. Some biologists believe that this difference is what makes grizzly mothers far more defensive around her cubs. A mother black bear will simply send her cubs up a tree, while the grizzly mother will hold her ground or attack.

- A bear's normal heartbeat on a summer day is 50–90 beats per minute. During hibernation, it only beats about 8 times a minute!

Thanks to Black Bears

- Besides being a prominent symbol of wild regions, many people enjoy seeing black bears in the wild.

- As omnivores, bears are members of the "cleanup crew" in the wilderness. They will not pass up the opportunity to scavenge on dead animals.

- Bears are an important component of the biodiversity of the Rocky Mountain region.

Myth Busters

MYTH: If you encounter a black bear, particularly a mother and cubs, you will be attacked.

There is a common legend that black bears, especially black bear mothers, attack any humans they see. That's simply not true. Black bears very rarely attack. It's highly unlikely that they will attack you, even if you are near a mother and her cubs. But that doesn't mean you should take the chance. If you see any black bears, keep to a safe distance. They may be shy, but they are still powerful creatures.

MYTH: When a black bear stomps its feet and bluffs a charge, it is preparing to attack.

Their most common aggressive displays are merely rituals that they perform when they are nervous; this includes fake charges. It's far more likely that bears will run away or seek safety in a tree.

MYTH: The best protection in grizzly country is a high-powered gun.

Records consistently show that people who defend themselves with pepper spray receive fewer injuries than those who defend themselves with a firearm. A recent study of 258 bear/human incidents in Alaska involving firearms found that firearms were effective in only 68 percent of the cases. This means that firearms were not effective for more than a third of the encounters. On the other hand, bear pepper spray was effective in 94 percent of 75 incidents in Alaska where pepper spray was employed. This makes sense upon further

black bear

consideration; with a gun you generally have 1 shot (or at the most, a few) under intensely stressful conditions. Pepper spray covers a wider area, increasing the likelihood it'll deter the bear.

Why They Bite

It's highly unlikely that you'll be bitten by a black bear. If bears have any impact on you at all, it's far more likely that bears will damage your campsite, camping gear, bird feeding station, garden or beehives. A friend who lived in grizzly and black bear country always liked to see a summer of good wild berry production. He would always say, "Good berries mean the bears are happy." Bears are essentially eating machines, and they need to put on amazing fat reserves for the upcoming winter. When natural foods, such as berries are scarce, bears become bolder and are attracted to our foods and gardens. Unfortunately, this often results in more human/bear conflicts and consequently it means more bruins are killed as nuisance bears.

How They Bite

Black and grizzly bears have powerful jaws with a full set of teeth, and they also have sharp claws, particularly on their front feet. These tools not only help them eat a wide range of foods, but they can serve as weaponry if needed. It should be noted, however, that most bear-related injuries are not major life-threatening episodes.

How Afraid Should I Be?

It's very unlikely that you'll be on the receiving end of a bear bite. You are far more likely to get killed riding your bicycle or drowning while swimming—and these are considered healthy pastimes.

Interestingly, an average of 1 person is killed in the United States each year by bears of all species. In contrast, white-tailed deer are responsible for more than 150 human deaths each year (deer/car collisions), and dogs kill an average of 15–20 people a year in our country. The reality is that the media seems to thrive on large animal attacks—while joggers and cyclists who encounter "attacks" from motorists rarely get the same onslaught of news coverage.

Preventing Black Bear Bites

- Remember, food is the primary reason that bears and humans encounter each other. Keep a clean campsite to minimize bear conflicts. Do not keep food scraps or garbage sitting out and don't dump them near your campsite. Don't clean fish or game near your camp.

- Whether you are car camping or primitive camping, keep all your food sealed in airtight containers or plastic bags to minimize bear encounters. And do all your food prep and cooking well away from your tents.

- The best protection in grizzly or black bear country is awareness of bears and their behavior. Watch for signs of bears in order to avoid encounters, and be sure to understand the defensive behaviors of bears (such as a bluff charge). This will help avoid an ugly bear encounter.

- When hiking in bear country it is best to hike in groups of 4 or more. And be talkative or sing songs. The idea is to never surprise a bear. Tim Rubbert, author of *Hiking with Grizzlies*, suggests, "Making the right noise in the right situation is probably the most important tactic for avoiding a bear encounter." By avoiding a close encounter, you will eliminate most bear problems.

- Never camp in areas where there is evidence of bears feeding nearby. Such clues might include torn-up logs or ant mounds, the smell of carrion or signs of bear diggings. Also, avoid camping in areas where you find bear droppings; particularly those that contain bits and pieces of plastic or paper packaging.

- If a bear approaches your camp, it is best if you and any others with you can appear as a mob of humans and make noise. This means yelling and banging pots and pans. But keep your distance and allow the bear an avenue of escape.

- Sometimes black bears will bluff charge. In such cases, the bear starts to charge, but then stops suddenly. If this happens, stand your ground, then back away slowly, talking calmly.

THINK TWICE

Think twice about setting up your picnic or camp near garbage cans or other human refuse.

Think twice before trying to get photo of a "cute" campground bear. Black bears that are used to people cannot be trusted.

- In some areas in bear country, campsites have metal bear-proof lockers for food storage. Properly hanging your food out of reach of bears can also protect it (and you). The U.S. Forest Service recommends that you hang food at least 12 feet off the ground and 10 feet away from the nearest tree trunk.

IF ATTACKED . . .

- If you have a firearm, use it as a last resort. If you have pepper spray, be sure to use it according to directions, and remember the broadcast spray is most effective at 10–15 feet, so don't spray it too early.

- NEVER run away or scream. Your fleeing might only trigger a more aggressive attack.

- If a black bear attacks you, it is best to aggressively fight back. If a grizzly bear actually attacks you, play dead AFTER it makes contact.

PEPPER SPRAY USE AGAINST AGGRESSIVE BEARS

Ideally, if you are well versed about bears, you will never have to use pepper spray. The main ingredient in the cloud of dispersed bear spray is a derivative of capsicum, an oil derived from red peppers. It affects the upper respiratory system and triggers an intense burning sensation in the eyes. Always buy spray that is labeled "bear deterrent spray."

Treatment of Bites

If you or someone in your party receives a bear bite or is scratched by a bear's claws, first determine the severity of the injury.

- Clean all non-life-threatening injuries and seek medical attention. Even if the wound is superficial, it is wise to seek medical assistance to help properly clean the wound.

- If there is abundant bleeding, apply pressure to the wound and call 911 for medical assistance.

BOTTOM LINE

It is highly unlikely that a black bear will attack you. Humans attack and kill their fellow humans at a rate more than 90,000 times that of bears harming us. Enjoy seeing these amazing animals, but stay a safe, nonthreatening distance away. Food is the primary reason bears cause problems for humans (such as tipped-over garbage cans or ransacked camps). Keeping a clean yard and campsite will greatly reduce the likelihood of bear problems.

Glossary

alpha a socially dominant individual; in the case of a wolf pack, the alpha pair is the socially dominant male and female breeding pair (pg. 129)

anaphylactic shock an extreme, often life-threatening, allergic reaction to an antigen (e.g., a bee sting) to which the body has become hypersensitive following an earlier exposure (pp. 10, 71)

anticoagulant a substance with the ability to slow or inhibit the clotting of blood (pp. 33, 39, 51, 75, 99)

bacterium a member of a large group of single-celled microorganisms that have cell walls but lack specialized structures and a nucleus; some, not all, can cause disease (pp. 26–28, 75)

carnassials the large upper premolar and lower molar teeth of a carnivore, adapted for shearing/cutting flesh (pp. 106, 119, 126, 131, 136)

carnivore an animal that eats other animals (pp. 106, 119, 126, 131, 136)

cephalothorax the fused head and thorax of spiders (pp. 43, 47)

chelicerae a pair of appendages, appearing like legs, that are found in front of the mouth of spiders and other arachnids; they are usually pincerlike claws (pg. 45)

clitellum a raised band that encircles the body of a worm and some leeches; it is made up of reproductive segments (pg. 73)

compound eye an eye consisting of many small visual units, typically found in insects and crustaceans such as certain shrimp (pg. 50)

DEET an abbreviation for an insect repellent called N,N-diethyl-meta-toluamide, a colorless, oily liquid with a mild odor; the chemical effectively "blinds" the insect's senses, so the biting/feeding instinct is not triggered (pp. 15, 28, 34, 40)

delayed fertilization a significant delay (longer than the minimum time required for sperm to travel to the egg) between copulation and fertilization; used to describe female sperm storage (pg. 83)

dermatitis a condition of the skin in which it becomes red, swollen and sore, sometimes with small blisters, resulting from irritation of the skin such as an allergic reaction (pg. 34)

echolocation the location of objects by reflected sound (echo), particularly used by dolphins, whales and bats (pp. 84–85, 87)

ecdysis when an organism, such as a rattlesnake, sheds its skin (pg. 91)

EpiPen a combined syringe and needle that injects a single dose of medication to counteract anaphylactic shock (pp. 10, 61, 67, 71)

estrus a period of fertility when many female mammals are receptive to sexual intercourse (pp. 123, 134)

exoskeleton a hardened or rigid external body covering found on some invertebrate animals; it provides both support and protection (pp. 30, 65)

hemolymph the fluid found in insects and other invertebrates that is similar to blood (pg. 14)

hermaphrodite an animal that possesses both male and female sex organs or other sexual characteristics; this might be abnormal or, in the case of earthworms, perfectly normal (pg. 73)

hibernation a physical condition of dormancy and inactivity that is an effective strategy for conserving energy during weather extremes such as winter; the metabolism is greatly reduced, often resulting in a lower body temperature, slower breathing and reduced heart rate (pp. 83–84, 113, 140–141)

Jacobson's organ a scent organ commonly found on the roof of the mouth of snakes and lizards (pg. 99)

lancet a small double-edged knife or blade with a sharp point (pp. 58–50)

Lyme disease a bacterial infection caused by the bite of an infected tick (pp. 23, 25–29)

larva the immature form of an insect (pp. 13–14, 17–19, 23, 31–32, 37–38, 50–51, 55, 57, 63, 121)

metamorphosis the transformation or change from an immature form to a completely different adult form; common in insects (pg. 13)

neurotoxin a poison or toxin that affects the nervous system (pg. 27)

omnivore an animal that eats both plants and other animals (pp. 105, 111, 117, 139, 141)

ovipositor the slender, tubular organ through which a female insect deposits eggs (pp. 57–58)

ovulate the release of ova (egg cells) from the ovary (pg. 83)

parasite an organism that gains nourishment from others (pp. 18, 73)

pedipalps specialized appendages, resembling legs, that are attached to an arachnid's cephalothorax; in scorpions, they are pincers; in spiders, they are sensory organs (pp. 43, 77, 79)

permethrin a synthetic insecticide of the pyrethroid class, used primarily against disease-carrying insects (pp. 28, 40)

pheromone a chemical substance that triggers a natural behavioral response in another member of the same species (pp. 43, 77)

pupa an insect in its inactive immature form, between larva and adult, such as in the chrysalis stage (pp. 13–14, 31, 32, 37, 50, 55, 63)

rabies a viral disease that invades the central nervous system of mammals, including humans (pp. 10–11, 85–87, 107, 109, 119, 120–121, 126)

spermatophore a protein capsule containing a mass of spermatozoa, which is transferred during mating in various insects, arthropods and some mollusks (pg. 77)

spirochete a flexible, spiral-shaped bacterium (pp. 26–27)

stylostome the channel-like structure that is formed by chiggers when feeding on a host's surface (pp. 18–19)

vasodilator an agent that helps with the opening or dilation of the blood vessels, which decreases blood pressure (pg. 74)

viable a seed, egg or embryo that is capable of growing and developing (pg. 51)

viviparous bringing forth live young that have developed inside the body of the parent (pp. 78, 91)

West Nile Virus a viral disease contracted through the bite of a mosquito; the disease interferes with the central nervous system and causes inflammation of brain tissue (pg. 39)

References

NO-SEE-UMS

"Biting Flies." Koehler, Philip G. and F. M. Oi. Institute of Food and Agricultural Sciences Extension, #ENY-220, April 1991. University of Florida, Electronic Data Information Source: http://edis.ifas.ufl.edu/ig081

"Biting Midges." Rutledge-Connelly, C. Roxanne. Featured Creatures, EENY-349, May 2005. University of Florida: http://entnemdept.ufl.edu/creatures/aquatic/biting_midges.htm

"Bluetongue Virus." McDill, Lisa. Indiana Animal Disease Diagnostic Laboratory, Spring 2002 Newsletter. Purdue University: http://www.addl.purdue.edu/newsletters/2002/spring/bluetongue.shtml

"Ceratopogonidae." Wikipedia, The Free Encyclopedia: http://en.wikipedia.org/wiki/Ceratopogonidae

McCafferty, W. Frank. *Aquatic Entomology: The Fishermen's Guide and Ecologists' Illustrated Guide to Insects and Their Relatives.* Jones and Bartlett Publishers, 1991.

"Sand Fly - No Seeum Control." U-Spray, Inc.: http://www.bugspray.com/article/sandflies.html

CHIGGERS

"Biology and Control of Chiggers." Cilek, James E. and Eric T. Schreiber. Public Health Entomology Research and Education Center, *EntGuide*, EG#6. Florida A&M University: http://pherec.org/EntGuides/EntGuide6.pdf

"Chigger." Study of Northern Virginia Ecology, Island Creek Elementary School. Fairfax County Public Schools: http://www.fcps.edu/islandcreekes/ecology/chigger.htm

"Chiggers." Koehler, Philip G. and F. M. Oi. Institute of Food and Agricultural Sciences Extension, #ENY-212, May 1991. University of Florida, Electronic Data Information Source: http://edis.ifas.ufl.edu/IG085

"Chiggers." Moore, Glen C. and M. E. Merchant. AgriLife Extension, E-365, November 2005. Texas A&M University: http://insects.tamu.edu/extension/publications/epubs/e-365.cfm

"Chiggers: Description of Chiggers, Elimination of Chiggers." Professional Pest Control Products: http://www.pestproducts.com/chiggers.htm

"Chiggers in Florida." Wild Florida Ecotravel Guide: http://www.wildflorida.com/articles/Chiggers_in_Florida.php

"Mystery Bites and Itches - Arthropod and Non-Arthropod Sources in Colorado." Cranshaw, Whitney S. Colorado State University Extension: http://www.ext.colostate.edu/pubs/insect/bug_bites.html

TICKS

"About Human Anaplasmosis." Minnesota Department of Health: http://www.health.state.mn.us/divs/idepc/diseases/anaplasmosis/basics.html

"Advanced Topics in Lyme Disease: Diagnostic Hints and Treatment Guidelines for Lyme and other Tick Borne Illnesses." Burrascano, Joseph J. Jr., M.D. "Managing Lyme Disease, Fifteenth Edition," September 2005. International Lyme and Associated Diseases Society: http://www.ilads.org/files/burrascano_0905.pdf

Article about Lyme disease in Montana from the *Missoulian*, March 2004. Merriam, Ginny. Canadian Lyme Disease Foundation. CanLyme: http://www.canlyme.com/montanalyme.html

"Blacklegged Tick or Deer Tick." Patnaude, Michael R. Featured Creatures, EENY-143, July 2000. University of Florida: http://entnemdept.ufl.edu/creatures/urban/medical/deer_tick.htm

"Colorado Tick Fever." Bureau of Epidemiology, August 2001. Utah Department of Health: http://health.utah.gov/epi/fact_sheets/ctf.html

"Colorado Tick Fever." MedlinePlus: http://www.nlm.nih.gov/medlineplus/ency/article/000675.htm

"Deer Ticks and Lyme Disease on Cape Cod and the Islands." Brochure provided by Barnstable County Department of Health and the Environment, Barnstable, MA.

Drummond, Roger. *Ticks And What You Can Do About Them.* Wilderness Press, 1990.

"Evaluation of a Tick Bite for Possible Lyme Disease." Sexton, Daniel J. UpToDate, Inc.: http://www.uptodate.com/contents/evaluation-of-a-tick-bite-for-possible-lyme-disease?

Guilfoile, Patrick. *Ticks Off! Controlling Ticks That Transmit Lyme Disease on Your Property.* ForSte Press, Inc., 2004.

"How Can I Avoid Ticks Carrying Lyme Disease? Lake Home & Cabin Kit, Second Edition." University of Minnesota Extension Service Faculty, 2006. University of Minnesota Extension: http://4h.umn.edu/distribution/naturalresources/components/DD8241_8.pdf

"Idaho Tick Types." Lahl, Jennifer. eHow: http://www.ehow.com/list_6893024_idaho-tick-types.html

"Known Vectors That Transmit Lyme Disease are Ticks." Canadian Lyme Disease Foundation. CanLyme: http://www.canlyme.com/ticks.html

Knutson, Roger M. *Furtive Fauna: A Field Guide to the Creatures Who Live On You.* Penguin Books, 1992.

"Lots Of Links On Lyme Disease." Reocities: http://www.reocities.com/HotSprings/Oasis/6455/

"Lyme Disease." Shiel, William C. Jr., M.D., F.A.C.P., F.A.C.R. MedicineNet, Inc. WebMD: http://www.medicinenet.com/lyme_disease/article.htm

"Lyme Disease in Interior Western States." November 2010. The Kaiser Papers: http://lyme.kaiserpapers.org/lyme-disease-in-interior-western-states.html

"MedlinePlus." U.S. National Library of Medicine. National Institutes of Health: http://www.nlm.nih.gov/medlineplus/medlineplus.html

"Mosquito and Tick-Borne Diseases: Rocky Mountain Spotted Fever." Perlin, David, Ph.D. and Ann Cohen. *The Complete Idiot's Guide to Dangerous Diseases and Epidemics,* 2002. Infoplease: http://www.infoplease.com/cig/dangerous-diseases-epidemics/rocky-mountain-spotted-fever.html

"Rocky Mountain Spotted Fever." Colorado Department of Public Health and Environment, Disease Control and Environmental Epidemiology Division. Colorado, The Official State Web Portal: http://www.cdphe.state.co.us/dc/zoonosis/tick/rmsfinfo.html

"Rocky Mountain Wood Tick." Green Valley Pest Control: http://www.greenvalleypc.com/html/ticks/rocky.htm

"Signs and Symptoms of Lyme Disease." Centers for Disease Control and Prevention: http://www.cdc.gov/lyme/signs_symptoms/index.html

"Tickborne Disease & Daylight Savings Time Arrive Together in Montana." Montana Public Health, Vol. 2, Added Issue, April 2007. Internet Archive: http://ia600508.us.archive.org/4/items/2D9FD079-6FE7-40D0-AE35-F4251F74E076/2D9FD079-6FE7-40D0-AE35-F4251F74E076.pdf

"Tick-Borne Diseases in Montana." Montana Integrated Pest Management Center, Yard and Garden Weeds, Insects, Diseases, December 2001. Montana State University Extension: http://ipm.montana.edu/YardGarden/docs/ticks-insect.htm

"Tickborne Diseases of the U.S." Centers for Disease Control and Prevention: http://www.cdc.gov/ticks/diseases/

"Tick-Borne Diseases: Relapsing Fever." Colorado Department of Public Health and Environment, Disease Control and Environmental Epidemiology Division. Colorado, The Official State Web Portal: http://www.cdphe.state.co.us/dc/zoonosis/tick/relapinfo.html

"Tick Borne Relapsing Fever." Centers for Disease Control and Prevention: http://www.cdc.gov/ncidod/dvbid/RelapsingFever/index.htm

"Ticks." Foley, Ian A. Montana Fish, Wildlife & Parks. Montana's Official State Website: http://fwp.mt.gov/recreation/safety/wildlife/ticks/

"Ticks and Tick-borne Diseases." New Mexico Department of Health: http://www.health.state.nm.us/erd/HealthData/documents/Ticks_001.pdf

"Ticks in Colorado." Julian, Joe. Colorado Master Gardener, 2010. Colorado State University Extension: http://www.colostate.edu/Dept/CoopExt/4dmg/Pests/ticks.htm

"Tularemia." Health Beat. Illinois Department of Public Health: http://www.idph.state.il.us/public/hb/hbtulare.htm

"Utah Lyme Disease Support Group." About Lyme Disease. UtahLyme: http://www.utahlyme.org./

"With Warmer Days Coming, Residents Reminded to Avoid Ticks." News from Wyoming Department of Health, April 2010. Wyoming Department of Health: http://m.health.wyo.gov/news.aspx?NewsID=380

"Wyoming Department of Health Warns About Tick-Borne Diseases." May 2007. HighBeam Research: http://www.highbeam.com/doc/1P3-1269096921.html

BLACK FLIES

"Biting Flies." Cranshaw, Whitney S., Frank B. Peairs and B. Kondratieff. Fact Sheet No. 5.582, December 1996. Colorado State University Extension: http://www.ext.colostate.edu/pubs/Insect/05582.html

"Black Flies." Butler, J. F. and J. A. Hogsette, Featured Creatures, EENY-30, June 1998. University of Florida: http://entnemdept.ufl.edu/creatures/livestock/bfly.htm

Klots, Elsie B. *The New Field Book of Freshwater Life*. Putnam Publishing Group, 1966.

McCafferty, W. Frank. *Aquatic Entomology: The Fishermen's Guide and Ecologists' Illustrated Guide to Insects and Their Relatives*. Jones and Bartlett Publishers, 1991.

"Simulidae Behavior." Marchetti, Michael P. Marchetti's Aquatic Ecology Lab. California State University: http://www.csuchico.edu/~mmarchetti/FRI/simulidae/simulidaebehavior.html

MOSQUITOES

"Disease Maps." Eastern Equine Encephalitis Human 2011: Montana. U.S. Geological Survey: http://diseasemaps.usgs.gov/eee_mt_human.html

"Disease Maps." West Nile Virus Human 2011: Idaho. U.S. Geological Survey: http://diseasemaps.usgs.gov/wnv_id_human.html

"Mosquito Management (Supplement to Fact Sheet 5.526)." Peairs, Frank B. and Whitney S. Cranshaw. Colorado State University Extension: http://www.ext.colostate.edu/westnile/mosquito_mgt.html

Spielman, Andrew, Sc.D. and Michael D'Antonio. *Mosquito: A Natural History of Our Most Persistent and Deadly Foe.* Hyperion, 2001.

"Tips For Treating Mosquito Bites." Green, Alan, M.D. F.A.A.P. July 1998. Dr. Greene: http://www.drgreene.com

"West Nile Virus and Mosquito-Borne Viruses in Colorado: Frequently Asked Questions." Colorado Department of Public Health and Environment, Disease Control and Environmental Epidemiology Division. Colorado, The Official State Web Portal: http://www.cdphe.state.co.us/dc/zoonosis/wnv/westnilefaq.html

"What is West Nile Virus?" Preventive Health and Safety Division. Wyoming Department of Health: http://www.health.wyo.gov/phsd/skeeter/whatisWNV.html

"What's Eating You? — July - August 2001." Weber, Larry. *Minnesota Conservation Volunteer,* July–August 2001. Minnesota Department of Natural Resources: http://www.dnr.state.mn.us/young_naturalists/biting_bugs/index.html

Wolff, Theodore A. and Lewis T. Nielsen. *The Mosquitoes of New Mexico.* University of New Mexico Press, 2007.

SPIDERS

"Brown Recluse Spiders in Colorado: Recognition and Spiders of Similar Appearance." Cranshaw, Whitney S. Fact Sheet No. 5.607, February 2008. Colorado State University Extension: http://www.ext.colostate.edu/pubs/insect/05607.html

Correspondence with Dr. David B. Richman, College Professor and Curator of The Arthropod Museum at New Mexico State University, Email: rdavid@nmsu.edu

Correspondence with Dr. Paula E. Cushing, Director of the American Arachnological Society, Denver Museum of Nature & Science, 2001 Colorado Boulevard, Denver, CO 80205-5798, Phone: 303.370.6442

"How to Identify Spiders in Colorado." Boston, David. eHow: http://www.ehow.com/how_4547848_identify-spiders-colorado.html

"Montana Spiders and Arachnids." Montana State University Extension: http://diagnostics.montana.edu/spider/

"Mystery Bites and Itches - Arthropod and Non-Arthropod Sources in Colorado." Cranshaw, Whitney S. Colorado State University Extension: http://www.ext.colostate.edu/pubs/insect/bug_bites.html

"Myth: Idiopathic Wounds are Often Due to Brown Recluse or Other Spider Bites Throughout the United States." Vetter, Richard S. PubMed Central, *The Western Journal of Medicine,* Vol. 173, November 2000. National Center for Biotechnology Information: http://www.ncbi.nlm.nih.gov/pmc/articles/PMG1071166/

"Spiders." Akre, Roger D., Ph.D., E. Paul Catts, Ph.D. and A. L. Antonelli, Ph.D. Insect Answers, EB1548, November 1997. Washington State University Extension: http://cru.cahe.wsu.edu/CEPublications/eb1548/eb1548.html

"USA Spider Identification Chart." Termite: http://www.termite.com/spider-identification.html

"Venomous Spiders Found in Each State." George, David W. Venombyte: http://www.venombyte.com/venom/spiders/venomous_spiders_by_state.asp

DEER AND HORSE FLIES

"Bites and Stings." Professional Pest Control Products: www.pestproducts.com/bitesandstings.htm

"Biting Flies." Koehler, Philip G. and F. M. Oi. Institute of Food and Agricultural Sciences Extension, #ENY-220, April 1991. University of Florida, Electronic Data Information Source: http://edis.ifas.ufl.edu/ig081

"Horse and Deer Flies: Biology and Public Health Risk." Hill, Catherine A. and John F. MacDonald. Public Health, Department of Entomology, E-246-W. Purdue Extension, Purdue University: http://extension.entm.purdue.edu/publications/E-246.pdf

Klots, Elsie B. *The New Field Book of Freshwater Life.* Putnam Publishing Group, 1966.

"Learn to Live With and Respect Horse Flies and Deer Flies." Murphree, Steve. *The Tennessee Conservationist*, Vol. LXXII, No. 4, July/August 2006. The Tennessee Conservationist, Tennessee Government: http://www.tn.gov/environment/tn_consv/archive/flies.pdf

McCafferty, W. Frank. *Aquatic Entomology: The Fishermen's Guide and Ecologists' Illustrated Guide to Insects and Their Relatives.* Jones and Bartlett Publishers, 1991.

HORNETS AND HONEYBEES

"Ants, Bees, and Wasps." Household and Pantry Pests, Fact Sheets. Virginia Tech: http://www.insectid.ento.vt.edu/fact-sheets/household-pantry-pests/index.html

"Controlling Bald-faced Hornets and Yellowjackets in and Around Structures." Bambara, Stephen B. and Michael Waldvogel. Residential, Structural and Community Pests, Insect Note - ENT/rsc-10. North Carolina State University: http://www.ces.ncsu.edu/depts/ent/notes/Urban/horn-yj.htm

Everett Clinic, The: http://www.everettclinic.com/health-library.ashx?1300/topic/symptom/insbt/overview.htm

"Foraging Yellowjackets." Potter, Michael F. College of Agriculture, Department of Entomology, Entfact-634. The University of Kentucky: http://www.ca.uky.edu/entomology/entfacts/ef634.asp

"How to Get Rid of Yellow Jackets / Yellow Jacket Control." Do-It-Yourself Pest Control: http://doyourownpestcontrol.com/yellowjackets.htm

"Paper Wasps and Hornets." Lyon, William F. and Wegner, Gerald S. Ohio State University Extension Fact Sheet, Entomology, HYG-2077-97. The Ohio State University: http://ohioline.osu.edu/hyg-fact/2000/2077.html

"Pollination." eBeeHoney: http://www.ebeehoney.com/Pollination.html

Scott, Susan and Craig Thomas, M.D. *Pests of Paradise: First Aid and Medical Treatment of Injuries from Hawaii's Animals.* University of Hawaii Press, 2000.

Stokes, Donald W. *A Guide to Observing Insect Lives: Stokes Nature Guides.* Little, Brown and Company, 1983.

GIANT WATER BUGS

"Beneficial Bugs." Eduwebs: http://www.eduwebs.org/bugs/bugindex.htm

"(Epinephrine) Auto-Injectors 0.3/0.15 mg." EpiPen: http://www.epipen.com

"Invasion of the Giant Water Bug, The." Leary, Alex. *St. Petersburg Times*, Tampa Bay, June 2003. St. Petersburg Times: http://www.sptimes.com/2003/06/21/Tampabay/The_invasion_of_the_g.shtml

"Pest Diagnostic Clinic Factsheet Archive." Laboratory Services Division. University of Guelph: http://www.uoguelph.ca/pdc/Factsheets/FactsheetList.html#Insect

LEECHES

"Facts About Leeches (Phylum Annelida, Class Hirudinea)." Skeel, M.E. Zoology, January 2009. Helium: http://www.helium.com/items/1283779-what-are-leeches

"Leeches and Clitellates: Phylogeny." Siddall, Mark E. The Leech Lab, Laboratories of Phylohirudinology. American Museum of Natural History: http://research.amnh.org/users/siddall/leechindex.html

"Natural History of Leeches (Annelida: Hirudinea)." Ginsberg, David and Dr. Jack Burch. University of Michigan Biological Station, Summer 1998. U-M Personal WWW Server: http://www-personal.umich.edu/~davegins/leech.html

"Picturing Science On View June 25." News, June 2011. American Museum of Natural History: http://www.amnh.org/news/tag/mark-siddall/

"Slippery Slope of Leech-Seeking, The: A Museum Curator Takes to the Field to Solve Some Mysteries of Leech Evolution." Cooper, Henry S. F. Jr. *Natural History*, November 2002. CBS Interactive Business Network Resource Library: http://findarticles.com/p/articles/mi_m1134/is_9_111/ai_93611615/

"Taste for Blood, A." Angier, Natalie. Science, October 2008. The New York Times: http://www.nytimes.com/2008/10/21/science/21blood.html

SCORPIONS

Correspondence on 11/18/10 with Dr. David B. Richman, College Professor and Curator of the Arthropod Museum at New Mexico State University, Email: rdavid@nmsu.edu

"Scorpions of The USA: Checklists by State." McWest, Kari J. Kari's Scorpion Pages: http://www.angelfire.com/tx4/scorpiones/states.html

BATS

Adams, Rick A. *Bats of the Rocky Mountain West: Natural History, Ecology, and Conservation*. University Press of Colorado, 2004.

"Bats of Colorado." Colorado Bat Working Group. Colorado State University: http://www.cnhp.colostate.edu/teams/zoology/cbwg/batList.asp

"Bats of Utah, The: A Literature Review." Oliver, George V. State of Utah, Department of Natural Resources, Division of Wildlife Resources—Utah Natural Heritage Program, Publication No. 00–14, April 2000. Utah DNR: http://www.dwrcdc.nr.utah.gov/ucdc/viewreports/bats.pdf

Wilson, Don E. *Bats in Question: The Smithsonian Answer Book*. Smithsonian Institution Press, 1997.

SNAKES

"Checklist of Idaho Reptiles." Peterson, Charles R. June 1997. Idaho State University: http://www.isu.edu/~petechar/idar/idahoreptileschecklist.html

"Checklist of Montana Amphibians and Reptiles Amphibians." Faculty Web Pages. Montana State University Billings: http://www.msubillings.edu/ScienceFaculty/handouts/Spring%202006/Barron/Biol%20460/Checklist%20of%20Montana%20Amphibians%20and%20Reptiles.pdf

Colorado Herpetological Society: http://www.coloherps.org/

"Colorado's Snakes." Colorado Herpetological Society: http://www.coloherps.org/reference/sort_snakes.htm

"Coping With Snakes." Cerato, M. and W. F. Andelt. Fact Sheet No. 6.501, May 2006. Colorado State University Extension: http://www.ext.colostate.edu/pubs/natres/06501.html

"*Crotalus viridis*: Western Rattlesnake." Valle, Laura. University of Michigan Museum of Zoology. Animal Diversity Web: http://animaldiversity.ummz.umich.edu/site/accounts/information/Crotalus_viridis.html

"Eastern Massasauga Rattlesnake: Why Conserve a Venomous Snake?" Endangered Species, Midwest Region, November 1999. U.S. Fish & Wildlife Service: http://www.fws.gov/midwest/endangered/reptiles/conserve.html

"Fast Facts: Prairie Rattlesnake." Animal Facts, Kids. Canadian Geographic: http://www.canadiangeographic.ca/kids/animal-facts/prairie_rattlesnake.asp

"List of Standard English and Current Scientific Names: Amphibians and Reptiles of New Mexico." Painter, Charles W. and James N. Stuart. University of New Mexico, Division of Amphibians & Reptiles, March 2004. Museum of Southwestern Biology: http://www.msb.unm.edu/herpetology/.../NM_species.htm

"Massasauga Rattlesnake." Dutton, Ian. Reptiles & Amphibians, October 2010. Suite101: http://www.suite101.com/content/massasauga-rattlesnake-a292700

"Modern Checklist of the Amphibians, Reptiles, and Turtles of Utah, A." Shofner, Ryan M. *Journal of Kansas Herpetology*, No. 21, March 2007. The Center for North American Herpetology: http://www.cnah.org/pdf_files/685.pdf

"*Sistrurus catenatus tergeminus*: Western Massasauga." Snakebook. National Natural Toxins Research Center: http://ntrc.tamuk.edu/specieshtm/sctergeminus.htm

"Venomous Snakes of Colorado." P.R.E.S.E.R.V.E.: http://www.preservevenomous.com/Venomous_Snakes_of_the_United_States/Venomous%20Snakes%20of%20Colorado/Venomous_snakes_of_Colorado.htm

Poole, Robert W. R. Nearctica.com, Inc.: http://www.nearctica.com/herps/snakes/viper/Catrox.htm

Poole, Robert W. R. Nearctica.com, Inc.: http://www.nearctica.com/herps/snakes/viper/Cvirid.htm

Poole, Robert W. R. Nearctica.com, Inc.: http://www.nearctica.com/herps/snakes/viper/Scaten.htm

SKUNKS
"Skunk (Mepitidae)." Lamb, Annette and Larry Johnson. Living Things, May 2002. Eduscapes: http://eduscapes.com/nature/skunk/index1.htm

"Skunks." Wildlife Species. Colorado Division of Wildlife: http://wildlife.state.co.us/WildlifeSpecies/Profiles/Mammals/Skunk.htm

SNAPPING TURTLES
"Reptile Description: *Chelydra serpentina*, Snapping Turtle." Northern Rockies Natural History Guide. The University of Montana – Missoula: http://nhguide.dbs.umt.edu/index.php?c=reptiles&m=desc&id=12

"Spiny Softshell - *Apalone spinifera*." Montana Field Guide. Montana's Official State Website: http://fieldguide.mt.gov/detail_ARAAG01030.aspx

"Spiny Softshell: *Apalone spinifera*." State of Utah Natural Resources, Division of Wildlife Resources. Utah DNR: http://dwrcdc.nr.utah.gov/rsgis2/Search/Display.asp?FlNm=apalspin

RACCOONS

"*Baylisascaris procyonis*: An Emerging Helminthic Zoonosis." Sorvillo, Frank, Lawrence R. Ash, O. G. W. Berlin, JoAnne Yatabe, Chris Degiorgio and Stephen A. Morse. Emerging Infectious Diseases, *EID Journal*, Vol. 8, No. 4, April 2002. Centers for Disease Control and Prevention: http://wwwnc.cdc.gov/eid/article/8/4/01-0273_article.htm

COYOTES

"Coyote Management: A Rationale For Population Reduction." Wade, Dale A. DigitalCommons@ University of Nebraska - Lincoln, Wildlife Damage Management, Internet Center for Great Plains Wildlife Damage Control Workshop Proceedings, October 1981. University of Nebraska, Lincoln: http://digitalcommons.unl.edu/cgi/viewcontent.cgi?article=1146&context=gpwdcwp

"Coyote Threat Reaches 'Fever Pitch': DOW Reports 'Tsunami' of Calls." Denver News, February 2009. ABC 7 News: http://www.thedenverchannel.com/news/18693976/detail.html

Hatler, David F., David W. Nagorsen and Alison M. Beal. *Carnivores of British Columbia: Royal BC Museum Handbook.* Royal British Columbia Museum, 2008.

"Take Action! Urge Greenwood Village (CO) to Adopt an Ecologically and Ethically Sound Coyote Management Plan." Action Alert, May 2009. Project Coyote: http://www.projectcoyote.org/newsreleases/news_greenwood.html

GRAY WOLVES

"Daniel Pletscher, Professor of Wildlife Biology, Director of the Wildlife Biology Program." College of Forestry and Conservation, Faculty. The University of Montana: http://www.cfc.umt.edu/PersonnelDetail.aspx?id=1138

"Experts Reassure Public Following Rare Fatal Wolf Attack." Teaching the World about Wolves, News & Events, December 2005. International Wolf Center: http://www.wolf.org/wolves/news/2005releases/123005_wolfattack.asp

"Frequently Asked Questions about Wolves." Teaching the World about Wolves, Basic Wolf Information. International Wolf Center: http://www.wolf.org/wolves/learn/basic/faqs/faq.asp#17

Interview on 10/27/10 with Dr. Daniel Pletscher, Professor of Wildlife Biology, Director of the Wildlife Biology Program, Department of Ecosystem and Conservation Sciences, The University of Montana.

"Gray Wolf Populations in the United States, 2006." U.S. Fish & Wildlife Service: http://www.fws.gov/home/feature/2007/gray_wolf_factsheet_populations.pdf

"News, Information and Recovery Status Reports." Gray Wolves in the Northern Rocky Mountains, Mountain-Prairie Region. U.S. Fish & Wildlife Service: http://www.fws.gov/mountain-prairie/species/mammals/wolf/

"Rocky Mountain Wolf Recovery 2009 Interagency Annual Report." Gray Wolves in the Northern Rocky Mountains, Mountain-Prairie Region. U.S. Fish & Wildlife Service: http://www.fws.gov/mountain-prairie/species/mammals/wolf/annualrpt09/

"Who's Afraid of the Big Bad Wolf?" -- Revisited." Mech, L. David. Teaching the World about Wolves, Basic Wolf Information. International Wolf Center: http://www.wolf.org/wolves/learn/basic/wolves_humans/perspectives/big_bad_wolf.asp

"Wolf Attacks on People." King, Nelson. Issues. Yellowstone Insider. http://www.yellowstoneinsider.com/issues/wolves/wolf-attacks-on-people.php

"Wolf Population & Distribution." Montana Fish, Wildlife & Parks. Montana's Official State Website: http://fwp.mt.gov/wildthings/management/wolf/population.html

"Wolves & Human Safety." Montana Fish, Wildlife & Parks. Montana's Official State Website: http://fwp.mt.gov/wildthings/management/wolf/human.html

"Wolves in Utah: An Analysis of Potential Impacts and Recommendations for Management." Switalski, T. Adam, Trey Simmons, Shiree L. Duncan, Andreas S. Chavez and Robert H. Schmidt. S. J. and Jessie E. Quinney Library, Natural Resources and Environmental Issues, Vol. X, 2002. Utah State University: http://www.cnr.usu.edu/quinney/files/uploads/NREIX.pdf

COUGARS

Busch, Robert H. *The Cougar Almanac: A Complete Natural History of the Mountain Lion.* The Lyons Press, 2004.

"Car Accident Statistics." Car-Accidents: http://www.car-accidents.com/pages/stats.html

"Claws." Cat Behavior. Animal Planet: http://animal.discovery.com/cat-guide/cat-anatomy/cat-claws.html

"Cougars on the Move." Kemper, Steve. *Smithsonian Magazine*, September 2006. Science & Nature, Smithsonian: http://www.smithsonianmag.com/science-nature/cougars.html

Hatler, David F., David W. Nagorsen and Alison M. Beal. *Carnivores of British Columbia: Royal BC Museum Handbook.* Royal British Columbia Museum, 2008.

Smith, Dave. *Don't Get Eaten: The Dangers of Animals that Charge or Attack.* Mountaineers Books, 2003.

BEARS

Anderson, Tom. *Black Bear: Seasons in the Wild.* Voyageur Press, 1992.

"Bear Spray vs. Bullets: Which Offers Better Protection?" Living with Grizzlies, Fact Sheet No. 8, Mountain-Prairie Region. U.S. Fish & Wildlife Service: http://www.fws.gov/mountain-prairie/species/mammals/grizzly/bear%20spray.pdf

Gookin, John and Tom Reed. *NOLS Bear Essentials: Hiking and Camping in Bear Country.* Stackpole Books, 2009.

Hatler, David F., David W. Nagorsen and Alison M. Beal. *Carnivores of British Columbia: Royal BC Museum Handbook.* Royal British Columbia Museum, 2008.

Herrero, Stephen. *Bear Attacks: Their Causes and Avoidance.* The Lyons Press, 1985.

Smith, Dave. *Don't Get Eaten: The Dangers of Animals that Charge or Attack.* Mountaineers Books, 2003.

RABIES

"Rabies." Centers for Disease Control and Prevention: http://www.cdc.gov/rabies/

"Rabies." Colorado Department of Public Health and Environment, Disease Control and Environmental Epidemiology Division. Colorado, The Official State Web Portal: http://www.cdphe.state.co.us/dc/zoonosis/rabies/index.html

"Rabies." Infectious Diseases. Eastern Idaho Public Health District: http://www.phd7.idaho.gov/Infectious%20Disease/Rabies/rabiesmain.html

"Rabies." Montana Fish, Wildlife & Parks. Montana's Official State Website: http://fwp.mt.gov/wildthings/livingWithWildlife/bats/bats_rabies.html

"Rabies: General Information." World Health Organization: http://www.who.int/rabies/epidemiology/Rabiessurveillance.pdf

"Rabies in Wyoming." Preventive Health and Safety Division. Wyoming Department of Health: http://www.health.wyo.gov/phsd/epiid/rabies.html

"Recent Evidence of Rabies in Montana Bats, Officials Warn." Department of Public Health & Human Services, July 2005. Montana's Official State Website: http://www.dphhs.mt.gov/newsevents/newsreleases2005/july/recentevidence.shtml

"To Help Deer—Don't Feed Them: Feeding Can Do More Harm Than Good." Wildlife Species. Colorado Division of Wildlife: http://wildlife.state.co.us/WildlifeSpecies/LivingWithWildlife/Mammals/

Photo credits by photographer and page number

Gary D. Alpert: 58

Scott Bauer/USDA Agricultural Research Service: 25 (black-legged tick)

Rick and Nora Bowers/www.BowersPhoto.com: 103 (western spotted)

J. F. Butler: 50

Kim A. Cabrera: 106

David Cappaert: 55 (paper wasp)

Mark Cassino: 51

Mary Clay/Dembinsky Photo Associates: 103 (eastern spotted)

Dan Downing: 27

Jerry W. Dragoo: 105

Dudley Edmondson: 97 (bull, garter, hognose)

Dr. Dennis Feely/University of Nebraska Medical Center: 25, 28 (electron microscope images of deer tick)

Tony Gallucci: 103 (hog-nosed)

James Gathany/CDC: 23 (all)

Christine Hass: 103 (hooded)

Tom Murray: 49 (both)

Gary Nafis: 97 (gopher)

Lee Ostrom: 46 (hobo)

Jerry A. Payne/USDA Agricultural Research Service, Bugwood.org: 55 (yellowjacket)

Phil Pellitteri: 56 (bottom)

Michael J. Plagens/www.arizonensis.org: 77

Corey Raimond: 112

Stan Tekiela: 97 (northern water), 98, 104, 111 (both)

About the Author

Tom Anderson is a professional naturalist, an award-winning writer and a wildlife expert. For 16 years he was director of the Lee and Rose Warner Nature Center, which is associated with the Science Museum of Minnesota and is located in Marine on St. Croix, Minnesota.

In addition to his work at the nature center, Tom is a well-known writer and columnist. For nearly 15 years he wrote "Reading Sign," an award-winning column for the *Chisago County Press*. He is also the author of 2 books, *Learning Nature by a Country Road* and *Black Bear: Seasons in the Wild*, both from Voyageur Press. He is a published poet and was a columnist for *Midwest Fly Fishing Magazine* and the Science Museum of Minnesota periodical, *Encounters*.

Tom has been honored many times for his writing. He was 1 of 20 Minnesota artists chosen to participate in the Millennium Journal Project. In 2003 he was awarded the "Best Commentary Award" by The National Association of Interpretation's magazine, *Legacy*. In 2004 he was runner-up for the "Best Feature" category.

The natural world and our intimate connection to it inspires Tom to write. He lives southwest of North Branch, but he travels often, especially in the far North. He lives with his lovely wife, Nancy Conger, in the nineteenth-century farmhouse that his Swedish great-great grandparents built.

Tom's website is www.aligningwithnature.com.